Archibald G. Kinloch, Scottland High Court of Justiciary

The trial of Sir Archibald Gordon Kinloch

For the Murder of Sir Francis Kinloch, bart., His Brother-German. Before the High

court of Justiciary on Monday June 29, 1795

Archibald G. Kinloch, Scottland High Court of Justiciary

The trial of Sir Archibald Gordon Kinloch
For the Murder of Sir Francis Kinloch, bart., His Brother-German. Before the High court of Justiciary on Monday June 29, 1795

ISBN/EAN: 9783337139445

Printed in Europe, USA, Canada, Australia, Japan

Cover: Foto ©Suzi / pixelio.de

More available books at **www.hansebooks.com**

THE

TRIAL

OF

SIR ARCHIBALD GORDON KINLOCH,

OF GILMERTON, BART.

FOR THE MURDER OF

SIR FRANCIS KINLOCH, Bart.

HIS BROTHER-GERMAN.

Before the High Court of Justiciary on Monday June 29. 1795.

TAKEN IN SHORT HAND,—AND CAREFULLY REVISED BY
THE COUNSEL.

EDINBURGH:

PRINTED BY C. DENOVAN,

FOR J. ELDER, NO. 9. NORTH BRIDGE, EDINBURGH,

AND G. G. AND J. ROBINSON, LONDON.

1795.

(v)

INDEX.

Debates

(vi)

THE
TRIAL
O F
Sir ARCH^{D.} GORDON-KINLOCH, Bart.

THE Prisoner was brought to the Bar a little before 10 o'clock.—He was dressed in black; and his demeanour was decent and respectful. He was attended by Sir Foster Cunliffe, Bart. his brother-in-law, and James Wilkie of Foulden, Esq; his cousin-german.

The Judges, in their Justiciary-robes, preceded by a Macer, bearing the Justiciary Mace, soon after took their places on the Bench in the following order, viz.

LORD JUSTICE CLERK,
Lord ESKGROVE,   Lord DUNSINNAN,
Lord SWINTON,   Lord CRAIG.

In support of the Prosecution, appeared

ROBERT DUNDAS, Esq; his Majesty's Advocate,
ROBERT BLAIR, Esq; Solicitor-General,
JOHN BURNET, Esq; Advocate,
Mr HUGH WARRENDER, Agent.

A   For

For the Pannel, appeared

DAVID HUME, Efq;
CHARLES HOPE, Efq;
WILLIAM RAE, Efq;
DAVID MONYPENNY, Efq;
} Advocates.

Meff. JAMES and CHARLES BREMNER, Agents.

Silence being proclaimed, the Clerk of Court ordered a Macer to call Robert Dundas, Efq; his Majefty's Advocate, for his Majefty's intereft, againft Major Sir Archibald Gord on-Kinloch of Gilmerton, Baronet; which being done with the ufual forms and folemnities, the Lord Juftice Clerk defired the Prifoner to attend to the Indictment then to be read.

INDICTMENT

" SIR ARCH^D. GORDON KINLOCH of Gilmerton, Baronet, prefent Prifoner in the Tolbooth of Edinburgh, You are Indicted and Accufed, at the inftance of ROBERT DUNDAS, Efq; of Arnifton, his Majefty's Advocate, for his Majefty's intereft, THAT WHEREAS, by the laws of God, the laws of this, and of every other well governed realm, MURDER, more efpecially when committed by a Brother againft a Brother, is a crime of a moft heinous nature, and feverely punifhable: YET TRUE IT IS, AND OF VERITY, That You, the faid Sir Archibald Gordon-Kinloch, are guilty actor, or art and part, of the forefaid crime, aggravated as aforefaid; IN SO FAR AS You, the faid Sir Archibald Gordon-Kinloch, being, on the 14th day of April 1795, in the houfe of Gilmerton, belonging to the deceafed Sir Francis Kinloch of Gilmerton, Baronet, Your Brothergerman, fituated in the parifh of Athelftonford, and county of Haddington, did, on the night of the faid 14th, or early in the morning of the 15th of April 1795, or on one or other of the days or nights of that month, or of the month of March immediately preceding, or of May
immediately

Immediately following, come down from your bed-chamber in the houfe of *Gilmerton* aforefaid, to the parlour or dining-room, where Your faid Brother then was, You having, at the time, two loaded piftols fome where concealed about Your clothes ; and having foon thereafter left the faid parlour or dining-room, and Your faid Brother having followed, and being then clofe by You, the faid Sir Archibald Gordon-Kinloch, on the ftair leading to the upper apartments, You did then and there Murder the faid Sir Francis Kinloch, Your Brother, by wickedly and felonioufly difcharging one of the faid loaded piftols at your faid Brother, by which he received a mortal wound ; the ball having penetrated below the point of the fternum or breaft-bone, towards the right fide : And the faid Sir Francis Kinloch having languifhed in great pain till the evening of the 16th of the faid month of April, did then expire, in confequence of the wound given him by You the faid Sir Archibald Gordon-Kinloch, and notwithftanding of every medical affiftance having been procured.— And You, the faid Sir Archibald Gordon-Kinloch, having, upon the 30th day of May 1795, been brought before James Clerk, Efq; Sheriff-depute of the fhire of Edinburgh, did, in his prefence, emit a Declaration, which was figned by You, the faid Sir Archibald Gordon-Kinloch : Which Declaration, together with two fmall pocket piftols, having the words " H. W. Mortimer, London, Gunmaker to his Majefty," marked on the barrel ; as alfo a piftol-ball, extracted from the body of the faid Sir Francis Kinloch ; as alfo a certificate dated at Gilmerton the 18th of April 1795, and figned " James Home, Benjamin Bell, G. Somner ;" alfo a letter from the deceafed Sir Francis Kinloch to Mr Alexander Frafer, Sheriff-clerk of Haddington, dated 15th of March 1795 ; another letter from the faid Sir Francis Kinloch to the faid Alexander Frafer without a date, but marked on the back 18th March 1795 ; as alfo a letter from You the faid Sir Archibald Gordon-Kinloch, to the faid Alexander Frafer, dated Haddington Jail, 22d day of April 1795 ; another letter from You the faid Sir Archibald Gordon-Kinloch to the faid Alexander Frafer, dated

the

the faid 22d day of April 1795; and alfo a letter, dated
Edinburgh Jail, 24th April 1795, from You the faid Sir
Archibald Gordon Kinloch, to the faid Alexander Frafer,
will all be ufed in evidence againft You, the faid Sir
Archibald Gordon-Kinloch, and will, for that purpofe, be
lodged in the hands of the Clerk of the High Court of
Jufticiary, before which you are to be tried, that you
may have an opportunity of feeing the fame. AT LEAST,
time and place above mentioned, the faid Sir Francis
Kinloch of Gilmerton was Murdered, and You, the faid
Sir Archibald Gordon-Kinloch, are guilty actor, or art and
part, of the faid crime. ALL WHICH, or part thereof,
being found proven by the verdict of an Affize, before the
Lord Juftice General, Lord Juftice Clerk, and Lords Commiffioners of Jufticiary, You the faid Sir Archibald Gordon-
Kinloch, OUGHT to be punifhed with the pains of law,
to deter others from committing the like crimes in all time
coming."*

Lord Juftice Clerk. Sir Archibald Gordon-Kinloch, Baronet, Are you Guilty or not Guilty?
Prifoner. Not Guilty.

After the Pannel had pled *Not Guilty,* Mr DAVID HUME,
one of his Counfel, addreffed the Court as follows:—
   My Lord Juftice Clerk,
   Your Lordfhips have heard the plea which the pannel
enters to the charge,— the grievous and too relevant
charge,—which is laid in this (as I muft needs admit it to
be) moft neceffary profecution againft him. And it now
remains for thofe who have undertaken the care of his
defence, (however unequal to fo important a tafk,) to explain to your Lordfhips, fomewhat more fully than the
pannel for himfelf can be expected to do, the meaning of
that plea, in the particular circumftances of this cafe; and
to point out to you the fcope and object of the proof in
exculpation, which is intended to be taken on his part.
   In pleading not guilty to the charge, the pannel would,
in the firft place, be underftood to intimate his denial of
that, which the profecutor in fupport of his libel has to
prove, and which, if he cannot prove, he muft fail in his
                                               profecution,

* Lifts of the Witneffes, cited on both fides, will be annexed.

profecution, namely, That it is He who has been the actor of the miferable deed of flaughter here related ;—a thing which, even if it be true, the pannel cannot confefs, having fcarce any knowledge or remembrance of what paffed on the occafion of himfelf, but from the relation of others only, which does not call for, nor would juftify a confeffion.

But farther, my Lord, and perhaps in this cafe ftill more material,—if unluckily it fhall appear and be fhewn, that the pannel's *hand* has been the unhappy caufe of the death of his Brother,—then, my Lord, and in that event, his plea muft be underftood to mean this other, equally available indeed, but far lefs fortunate defence, that at leaft his heart and purpofe have not been in the deed, but his hand only,—that it was not the work of malice and defign, (without which there is no murder,) but of pure fatality and misfortune, which he could not avoid, and for which he is not the object of punifhment, but of fympathy and commiferation:—Becaufe, my Lord, at the time ftated in this Indictment, the pannel was no longer to be numbered in the rank of reafonable and accountable beings, but by one of thofe high and dreadful vifitations of Providence, to which we *all*, the wifeft and the beft of us, are equally liable, and from which even thrones are not exempt, had been deprived of all felf-government,—of all regulation of his conduct, or controul of his paffions,—of all difcernment of friend from foe, or of that which was meant to ferve from that which was meant to harm him,—and acted, in fhort, under the blind impulfe of a diftempered and furious imagination, which tranfported him wherefoever it would,—which filled him with a thoufand vain jealoufies, horrors, and apprehenfions,—and would equally have turned his hand againft whatfoever perfon had at that moment come in the way. This, my Lord, is the pannel's plea and main reliance.

My Lord, while I ftate it for him, I am not ignorant of the reports and rumours that are abroad in the world; rumours, I am forry to fay, which, on the very day preceding this trial, and even from the pulpit, the feat itfelf of truth and of charity, have, in contempt of decency and humanity,

---

* A miftake in point of fact for the Sunday fe'enight before.

humanity, been induſtriouſly circulated to condemn him. I
ſay, I am not ignorant of theſe reports, and of the weight
of prejudice and ſuſpicion, with which, in conſequence, I
have to ſtruggle; not indeed with your Lordſhips, whoſe
breaſts are void of every feeling of the ſort, and who will
liſten to nothing but the information of the law, and the
ſtill voice of your own conſcience; but with the people at
large, from among whom the perſons, who as Jurymen are
to decide on the pannel's fate, are and muſt be taken. Nor,
my Lord, do I think it very wonderful, that ſuch ſhould be
their feelings on this extraordinary occaſion. My Lord,
when they are told the miſerable ſtory of this event,—that
a worthy and excellent gentleman,—the repreſentative of a
flouriſhing and reſpected family.—juſt arrived at the poſſeſ-
ſion of his inheritance, in the courſe of nature, by the death
of his aged father. (a father, in good time removed from
the fight of ſuch a ſcene among his children;)—when, my
Lord, they are told that this good and eſtimable perſon,
ſurrounded with all the fair proſpects of a long, a happy
and an uſeful life,—that he has been taken off by a foul Murder,—a murder committed under his own roof, almoſt at
his own table, and in the midſt of his domeſtics, friends and
relations; and when to all this it is added, that he has fallen by the hand of his own brother, his gueſt at the time,
and inmate of his houſe, by him " *who ſhould againſt the*
" *Murderer ſhut the door, not bear the knife himſelf:*"
No wonder, when this lamentable ſtory is related, if, in
the firſt emotions of pity and of indignation at ſo ſad
and ſtrange a tragedy, any thing that *can* be ſaid in
defence of the unhappy author of ſo much miſchief, is
heard at firſt with a cloſe heart and an unfavourable ear.

But, my Lord, how natural and how excuſeable ſoever
theſe emotions, (as ſurely they are *moſt* excuſeable,) they are
not, however, the juſt and proper emotions for this time
and occaſion; nor is this a diſpoſition which they can be ſuffer-
ed to bring with them into the preſence of this Court of Juſtice; into which, my Lord, they are not called to aſſuage
their paſſions, or indulge their feelings, with regard to an

event,

event, which, however deplorable, is paſt and gone, and
cannot be recalled, (I would it could;) but to try as
Judges, cooly and impartially to try, nay ſcrupulouſly and
tenderly to try, the manner of that calamity, whether it
was of chance or of deſign, and to decide on the life and
death of a frail and infirm mortal like themſelves, who
if, by the will of Providence, he has truly been viſited with
this grievous and ſore afflićtion, and has been the inſtru-
ment of deſtroying a brother, who never did him harm,
and whom he never regarded *but* as a brother, is himſelf
far more to be pitied than the deceaſed, and is no objećt
of judgement, but for that Almighty Judge whoſe hand hath
ſmitten him. Theſe things, I truſt and hope in God, that
all now preſent, and thoſe eſpecially who have been called to the office of Jurymen, will, as they value the intereſt
of juſtice, or their own peace of mind, remember and keep
in view; and that there are no bounds nor meaſure to the
idle, the confident, yet falſe and groundleſs ſtories which
a whole country, commenting upon one, and that ſo mar-
velous and intereſting a ſu j. ćt, muſt give riſe to.

My Lord, I aſk your Lordſhips pardon for juſt touching on this topic, unneceſſary I confeſs to your Lordſhips,
and to which I ſhall not again recur. With reſpećt to
the proper buſin. ſs before the Court,—in ſtating the pannel's plea in the general terms I have already uſed, I
have perhaps ſufficiently complied with the rule of Court,
and have ſtated *that,* which you cannot *but* ſuſtain as a
relevant and lawful defence. But, my L rd, from any
thing I know of this caſe, I ſhall have no objećtion to lay
the ſtate and hiſtory of the faćt ſomewhat more fully be-
ore the Court; though, on the other hand, it cannot, and
know will not be expećted of me, to enter into a diſqui-
tion concerning the nature of Madneſs, (the thing of
ll others the hardeſt to be deſcribed,) or that I ſhould attempt to aſcertain the peculiar claſs and charaćter of the
diſtemper, to which this unhappy man was liable.

Suffice it to ſay, that it was no ſhort, ſudden, and unaccountable fit of phrenzy, for the firſt time obſerved at the
moment

moment of the slaughter, (though, allow me to observe, even this, if absolutely and fully proved, would in law, as in reason, be sufficient;) but the pannel's plea is far more favourable. Upwards of fifteen years ago, I believe in 1779, when abroad in the West Indies, in the service of his country as an officer, the pannel had the misfortune to be seized with one of those dreadful fevers incident to the climates of that quarter of the world, and which raged with such violence at this time, that out of 5000 men, which composed their little army in the island of St. Lucia, no fewer than 1800 were, in the course of a few months, swept away. After a long and severe illness, and by the pure strength of his constitution, he escaped, my Lord, at last, with his life; but I cannot say, fortunately escaped, for he left the better part of him *behind*; and from thence forward was no longer the man he had been before. Not only, my Lord, was there a great alteration of the temper and humour of the man, who, from social, chearful, and good humoured, became sullen, jealous, and irascible, and extremely changeable and uncertain,— not only was there a decay of the vigour of his intellect—a confusion, weakness, and cloudiness of understanding; but there had come to be at times a plain derangement and disorder—and this to such a degree, as had on one occasion tempted him to turn his hand against his own life, (as he is now charged to have done against his brother's;)—and this an attempt of so violent and serious a nature, (by cutting himself very deeply in the wrist,) as occasioned him a confinement of three months, before he was again fit to come abroad.

This, my Lord, had been his state for years. But of late, and recently before the event which gives rise to this trial, things had plainly been verging, (as happens with this malady,) from worse to worse, into absolute insanity and deprivation of reason. Of which melancholy truth, my Lord, so much were all about him,—so much was the deceased himself convinced, (not to mention the many strong proofs of it that will be given you in his actions and con-

)

duct,) that every preparation had been made, the ftrait
waift-coat provided, a keeper engaged, and the proper attendants fummoned to the houfe, to reduce him,
by main force, into a ftate of coercion as a *madman*, who
could no longer be fuffered to go at large.

Happy would it have been for the deceafed, happy for the
pannel, for the common friends of the family, and for the
public, if this falutary, this neceffary purpofe, had with
due difpatch and refolution been carried into effect: For to
the undue delay of it, (owing, I admit, to amiable, but moft
unfortunate motives,) was the cataftrophe owing that en-
fued. Had it not been for that delay, and an aukward
and ill conducted attempt in the end to feize his perfon, at
a time, when there was no force at hand to mafter him,
Sir Francis Kinloch might now have been alive, and hap-
-py in the midft of his friends ;—your Lordfhips would
have been fpared this painful piece of duty ;—and Sir Archibald Gordon-Kinloch, a gentleman of birth and accom-
plifhments, and born to happier profpects, would not now
have ftood expofed, a public and miferable fpectacle, at
the bar of a Court of Juftice, and under trial for his
life.

My Lord, when I have explained the defence in thefe
terms,—a ftate of utter infanity, at the time of the deed,
and preceded by a courfe of infirmity and of occafional
derangement for years, I truft I have laid a plea
before you, which ftands in no need of aid from cafes,
books or precedents, to recommend it to the attention
and favour of the Court ; nor will I confume one moment of your Lordfhips time, which, I am afraid, will at
any rate be long encroached on, with the quotation of
any fuch, in fupport of that which nature, reafon, and
humanity prefcribe.

The Court delivered their opinions, which coincided
with the propofition of Mr Hume ; and the following
Interlocutor was pronounced :—

" The Lord Juftice Clerk, and Lords Commiffioners of
" Jufticiary, having confidered the criminal libel, raifed

" and

" and purfued at the inſtance of Robert Dundas, Eſq;
" of Arniſton, his Majeſty's Advocate, againſt the ſaid Sir
" Archibald Gordon-Kinloch of Gilmerton, Baronet, they
" find the libel relevant to infer the pains of law; but
" allow the pannel to prove all facts and circumſtances
" that may tend to exculpate him, or alleviate his guilt:
" And remit the pannel, with the libel, to the knowledge
" of an Aſſize."

The Jury being called, and no objection made to any
of them, the following gentlemen were impannelled:—

THE JURY.

1. Andrew Wauchope of Niddry Mariſchal, *Chancellor*.
2. John Wauchope of Edmonſtone.
3. George Ramſay of Whitehill.
4. Simon Fraſer of Ford.
5. Robert Trotter of Caſtlelaw.
6. John Newton of Curriehill.
7. Alexander Keith of Ravelſton.
8. George Ramſay younger of Barnton.
9. James M'Aulay druggiſt in Edinburgh.
10. Robert Sanderſon merchant there.
11. William Coulter merchant there.
12. Thomas Hutchiſon baker there.
13. John Moncrieff apothecary there.
14. Patrick Inglis merchant there.
15. Elphinſton Balfour bookſeller there, *Clerk*.

EVIDENCE FOR THE CROWN.

1. DUNCAN M'MILLAN, writer in Edinburgh, examined
by Mr BURNET.—Were you acquainted with the late Sir
Francis Kinloch? I was. Do you remember, on Monday
13th of April laſt, ſeeing Major, now Sir Archibald Gordon
Kinloch? Yes, I came from Edinburgh with Mr'Alexander Kinloch. Do you remember of meeting a chaiſe
on your road to Haddington? Yes. At what time might
this be? Paſt 3 o'clock in the afternoon. Did you ob-
ſerve who was in the chaiſe? The priſoner at the bar was
in

in it. Did you obferve any thing particular in his appearance? He threw himfelf back, as if wifhing to avoid being feen. Did the chaife ftop?—No.

Lord Juftice Clerk. Were you going in oppofite directions? Yes.

Mr Burnet. Had you any converfation with Mr Alexander Kinloch on this occafion? He expreffed furprife, becaufe he thought his brother had gone to London. Did Mr Alexander mention the day that he fuppofed his brother had gone to London?—No.

You paffed on to Haddington? Yes, and ftopped at Mrs Fairbairn's. Did you dine at Mrs Fairbairn's?—Yes. Had you any other company?—Yes, Mr George Somner, who dined with us. Did you fee Major Gordon-Kinloch there?—I heard the noife of a carriage,—I looked out at the window, and obferved that it was the fame chaife we had met.—It ftopped at Mr Somner's fhop.

Did you, or any of the company, go out?—Mr Somner went out, and returned foon after, with Major Gordon-Kinloch. Had you any converfation with the Major?—Yes.—I afked him how he was.—He anfwered, he was very ill. Did he continue in the room with you, or did he go out? He went out and returned again. How long did you remain in Fairbairn's houfe, and how did the Major behave when he returned? When he came back, we preffed him to take a glafs of wine and water; and he was in fo bad a ftate, that he was not able to carry it to his head.

Did you go to Gilmerton that night? Yes.—Who went along with you? Mr Alexander Kinloch. Had you not occafion to know that another perfon went along with Mr Somner? Mr Somner and the pannel fet out with the intention of going to Gilmerton, as they faid. Did they not go forward? The chaife, in which the pannel and Mr Somner were, ftopped at a place called *Cozburd-tail*, about a mile from Gilmerton. We afked them why they ftopped? And they faid, To make water.

Lord

Lord Justice Clerk. Mr Somner made the anſwer? Yes.

Mr Burnet. What paſſed further? After they had ſtopped a conſiderable time, I aſked What detained them ſo long? and Mr Somner anſwered, That the Major had gone away.— Was a poſtilion ſent after him? One of the poſtilions was ſent to look for him : He came back, and informed us, that he had overtaken the Major, who ſaid he was going to Haddington, where he ſaid he would be found. Did you then go on to Gilmerton? Yes, we arrived there a little after ten, at night. Did both chaiſes go on? Both. Do you remember of any thing being taken out of the chaiſe in which the Major was? I think there were ſome things taken out, but I was not preſent.— What happened after your arrival at Gilmerton relating to the Major? Mr Somner came into my bed-room in the morning, told me, that he was going to Haddington to look after the pannel, and deſired me to follow him as quickly as I could. You went to Hadington then? Yes, after breakfaſt, and enquired for the Major, but could get no information of him. Did you go back to Gilmerton that day? Yes, I returned before dinner. Was Sir Francis Kinloch at home? Yes; alſo Mr Alexander, Miſs Kinloch, and a Mr Low.

Do you remember any thing that happened after dinner? I remember there was a meſſage brought to me, that ſomebody wanted to ſpeak to me.—About what time was this? About half an hour after dinner.—When was dinner? We ſat down to dine about five.—Who was the perſon that wanted you? It was William Reid the gardener?—What paſſed between you? He told me that he had been up at Mr Walker's of Beanſton, and that he had ſeen the Major there, who was in a very diſagreeable ſituation indeed.—That he went up ſtairs, and knocked at the door where the pannel was.—That the pannel called out who was there, and the door was half-opened from within.—There was no body in the room but the pannel.—He had a piſtol in his hand, which alarmed Reid exceedingly.

Lord

Lord Juſtice Clerk. He had a piſtol you ſay?—Yes, my Lord.—This is all that William Reid told me.

Mr Burnet. How did you proceed? I called Sir Francis out of the room to inform him; and the pannel appeared ſoon after.—I obſerved him, before he came up to the houſe, from the window of the lobby.—Did he come into the houſe? Yes, he came into the lobby.— What converſation paſſed there? Very little.

Lord Advocate. Do you recollect any part of that converſation? His brother and I enquired how he did, and he ſaid, Very poorly.

Mr Burnet. Do you recollect where he went next? By the deſire of Sir Francis, who took him by the arm, he went to his own bed-chamber, and I returned to the dining-room. What happened next? A meſſage was ſoon after brought to Mr Low, that Sir Francis had been taken very ill, and could do no buſineſs that night; upon which Mr Alexander Kinloch left the dining-room, and went up ſtairs, and ſhortly after Mr Low went away. Had you occaſion to leave the dining-room, and go up ſtairs? Yes, to the Major's room. What converſation had you with the Major? I do not recollect. Was the Major in bed? He was lying on the bed, and part of his clothes were off. Do you recollect any converſation that paſſed? The Major ſpoke, and converſed a good deal with his brother Sir Francis; but I don't recollect the purport of the converſation. How long did you remain in the room? Not long.—I was there occaſionally.—The family went to ſupper about eleven, but the Major did not come down.— Was Sir Francis in the room? Yes.

Lord Advocate. You ſaw the pannel before at Fairbairn's, and afterwards at Gilmerton, Did he appear in a better or worſe ſituation at the latter period than at the former? He appeared a great deal calmer, from the attention of his brother Sir Francis. Do you recollect the ſubſtance of what paſſed in converſation? No. Did he hold any irrational or incoherent converſation, either in your or his brother's preſence before ſupper? I cannot ſay. Did any

thing

thing pafs, which imprefled your mind at the time, that
he was unfit to hold a rational converfation? I did not think
him perfectly collected. Was he more or lefs collected
than when you faw him at Fairbairn's? He was more collected.—From what circumftance or appearance did you
form this opinion, that he was not perfectly collected?
It was from his converfation.—He wandered from topic
to topic.

Mr Burnet. How long did the company fit at fupper?
Till three in the morning.—Did any perfon join them?
Yes, Mr George Somner. At what time did he come
there? Between 10 and 11. This was before fupper?
It was. At what time did you go to bed? Immediately
after fupper. Have you occafion to know, If Sir Francis
went to bed then? He left the room before I did go to
bed. He had occafionally left the dining-room in order
to vifit the Major. Did you fee him afterwards? I faw
him in his bed-chamber before I went to bed. What did
you fay to him? I advifed him to go to bed. How long
were you in bed? I was waked by Mr George Somner.
(*L. J. Clerk.* There was only one Mr Somner here? Yes.)
What was the occafion of Mr Somner waking you? To
tell me that Sir Francis was fhot. Where did you go
to? Straight to Sir Francis's room. In what fituation
did you find Sir Francis? The fervants were undreffing
him. Did he fpeak to you? He told me not to mind
him, for there were plenty with him; but to go and prevent his poor fifter from coming into the room. Did you
fee any wound about Sir Francis? I faw a wound, and
was defired by Mr Somner to put my hand upon it, to
prevent the external air from entering. Did you prevent Mifs Kinloch from entering the room? I went immediately to the door, when Sir Francis defired me, but
could not prevent her from coming in. She came in,
and was very much diftracted. Did fhe remain in the
room? No, we were forced to carry her out.—I returned, after feeing Mifs Kinloch to her room. Were any
exprefles fent off? There was an exprefs fent to Edinburgh

burgh for Doctor Monro and Mr Benjamin Bell, and another to Haddington, for Mr Richard Somner.——I then
went into the room where Sir Francis was, and support-
ed him for half an hour, while Mr George Somner was
preparing bandages.

Lord Advocate. Did any conversation pass between the
deceased and you on the subject of the event that had taken place? None, only he said, " God Almighty help that
" poor unhappy man." Did you, in passing from your
own apartment to that of Sir Francis, see the prisoner? No,
I did not see him again. Was he not on the stairs, nor in
the lobby? No. When did Mr Bell arrive? He came
about eleven o'clock. Was Sir Francis regularly attended by medical persons? Yes. Had you any farther conversation with Sir Francis? I had some little conversation,
but none on the accident, or the person who committed it, except what I mentioned before. How long did
Sir Francis survive the accident? The wound was received on Wednesday morning, and he died on Thursday
night, about eleven o'clock. —— You were intimate
in the family of the late Sir David Kinloch, How long did
that intimacy continue? From the year 1762. Were
you intimate from the year 1780 downwards? Yes.——
When did Sir David die? In February last. Was the
pannel at that time in the house? Yes. How long did
he continue after? I cannot say; I went away. Did Sir
Francis ever go from home at any time, and leave his
brother, his sister and you, at Gilmerton? Yes. I came
into Edinburgh before the Session rose, and before that
time, Sir Francis had gone to Edinburgh. Did you remain at Gilmerton during the time of Sir Francis's ab-
sence? Yes. Who acted as landlord then? The Major. During any time previous to the 12th of March,
Had you occasion to observe any thing particular in
the conduct of the prisoner? Nothing, except that he was
dissatisfied with his father's settlements. Does it consist
with your knowledge, that Sir Francis had any particular reason for going to Edinburgh. Yes, it was to take
the

the advice of counfel on his father's fettlements. Do you
not know, that it was on account of the diffatisfaction
that the pannel had expreffed? Yes, from the time that
Sir Francis left Gilmerton to go to Edinburgh, till the
day that the witnefs left it alfo. Did any converfation
pafs on that topic? Yes. What was the tendency of that
converfation? The pannel expreffed his diffatisfaction in
feveral converfations. From the year 1780 downwards,
Did you obferve any thing particular in the conduct of
the prifoner? He was remarkable for being exceedingly
troublefome when he got drink. Do you recollect any
other peculiarity? He was fometimes not correct, not fane.
Do you allude to the time he was in liquor or otherwife?
He was confined for infanity once in Edinburgh. Do you
recollect when? It was a few years ago. Is it from that circumftance, or any other, that you formed your opinion of
him being infane? It is from that circumftance, together with
other appearances. Of what nature were thefe other
appearances? That of being troublefome in company; and,
at a former period of life, he was one of the moft mild and
pleafant men in company I ever faw. Did you ever obferve any appearances, when fober, which could induce
you to fuppofe him infane? I remember once, fome years
ago, that he came to my bed-fide, in my own houfe, about
five in the morning, and faid, he was going to fet off for
Greenock to fee Major Mackay.

L. J. Clerk. Had he not been in town? No ; he had
been travelling all night. Was he fober? Yes.

Lord. Advocate. Was it from his converfation or appearance that you judged him infane? From both. Did he
tell you his purpofe in going to vifit Major Mackay?
No. Nor where he had been? Yes, at Berwick. Did you
attempt to diffuade him? Yes. Did he ftate any reafon
why he was going to fee Major Mackay? None. Did you
take any fteps in confequence of this? No. Did you ever
communicate to his family the opinion you had formed?
I think that I muft have mentioned to Sir Francis, that I
thought him infane.

Do

Do you know of any caufe of enmity, or of any grudge, fubfifting between the pannel and his brother? His conduct when in drink was very extraordinary. Do you remember any thing more remarkable than another? I remember very high words paffing between them, and the prifoner ftruck Sir Francis. Did Sir Francis give any caufe for this? He certainly was in a great paffion. Was there any caufe for this paffion? The pannel had given great abufe to a gentleman at his father's table, and Sir Francis reproved him for it. He ftruck him with a glafs tumbler, and wounded him upon the face. Were you prefent at the abufe that had taken place? I was. In your opinion, was the abufe fuch as to juftify Sir Francis for taking his brother to tafk? I think it was. What happened in confequence? I carried Sir Francis up ftairs and dreffed him. Sir David was not informed of it then? Not for fome time. Does it confift with your knowledge, that the pannel was obliged to leave his father's houfe on account of this mifunderftanding? I think he was. How did Sir Francis take this behaviour? He forgave him. He did not feel any refentment.

During the laft years of your acquaintance with the pannel, was he accuftomed to leave the houfe fuddenly, without warning, or telling where he was going? Yes. And did he come back, without telling where he had been? Yes. Were any fteps taken, or propofed to be taken to confine him? I never heard of any during all this time, till immediately before the prefent event. I mean till after Sir David's death.

Mr Burnet. Had you occafion to know that the Major came to Edinburgh, and refided there fome time before his brother's death? Yes. How long before his death? A few days, and he lived in the Black Bull Inn. In what ftate did he appear? Was he able to converfe on general fubjects? He was. Do you remember any difference in his appearance from what you had feen at Gilmerton? I thought he had been living harder then ufual. Did you obferve any other alteration? No.

C

(18)

Ld. Advocate. You tell us you never knew of any fteps being taken to confine him? None, until I went to Haddington. When? On the Monday evening. Was that the firft time? Yes. What induced the family to do this? The deranged ftate he was in. Were any fteps actually taken? Mr Somner returned from Gilmerton to Hadding-ton, for the purpofe. Was there any preparation made in the courfe of Tuefday? None, till Tuefday night. The pannel came home about Six, and Mr Somner was fent for about ten; and it was propofed to fe-cure the pannel, but Sir Francis delayed it. Who pro-pofed it? Sir Francis himfelf propofed it.

DUNCAN M'MILLAN, *crofs examined by Mr* HUME.— Deponed, That the pannel, when in Mrs Fairbairn's, at-tempted to fwallow a bit of meat, and could not: That his brother Alexander affifted him to carry the glafs to his head, on account of the fhaking of his hand: That he was unquiet and reftlefs; kept walking backwards and forwards through the room, and went out to the ftable-yard and garden: That he feemed oppreffed and unhappy, and hardly joined in the converfation: That he gave no reafon for his purpofe of going to Edinburgh, nor for returning to Haddington, nor for calling at Mr Somner's: That the agitation of his perfon, and the fhaking of his hand, appeared to the deponent to arife from illnefs, and not from liquor: That he did not prefs drinking, or fhow any defire for it; on the contrary, drank lefs than others of the company; and that, of courfe, they would not have affifted him to carry the glafs to his head, if they had thought that he had already got more than he was the better of: That Mr Som-ner gave directions to the hoftler to look after him, as ap-pearing to be ill and deranged, and unfit to take care of himfelf: That on the evening, when the pannel ftruck his brother, it was after fupper, and the bottle had been on the table, and the party drinking from dinner to fup-per: That, on the evening of Tuefday the 14th, Mr Som-

ner

ner had brought a ſtrait waiſt-coat with him to be put on
the pannel, and a nurſe or keeper to attend him.

Lord Juſtice Clerk. You have deponed to various
meetings with the pannel before the accident happened,
Now, according to beſt of your judgement, was he in a
capacity to know the difference between moral good and
evil, and to know that murder was a crime? I cannot
ſay. Say to the beſt of your judgment? I think he was
in a capacity to judge between good and evil.

Lord Eſkgrove. Had you any reaſon to believe, that
the priſoner was acquainted with the coming of the woman from Haddington? No.

Mr TROTTER, (*one of the Jury*), Did Sir Francis, after
coming out of the Major's room, on the night on which
the accident happened, ſpeak as if there had been any
difference that night between him and the Major?
No.*

GEORGE SOMNER, ſurgeon in Haddington, *examined by
Mr Solicitor-General* BLAIR.

Were you well acquainted with the deceaſed Sir Francis Kinloch? Yes. Do you remember of receiving a meſſage
from Gilmerton on Monday the 13th of April laſt? A
meſſenger came from Miſs Kinloch, deſiring the witneſs to come immediately and ſpeak to her. I went
there about one or two o'clock. What converſation
paſſed betwixt Miſs Kinloch and you? It was to prevent Major Kinloch from going to Edinburgh, for ſhe
thought him in a very unſettled ſtate of mind, and not fit
to undertake the journey. Did you ſee the Major? I
ſaw him before I ſaw Miſs Kinloch. He was in a poſt-
chaiſe at the door. He ſaid he was going to town. Did
he accordingly ſet out? Not immediately. I obſerved him
in the chaiſe very much agitated; and, from his appearance,
ſuſpected

* It was underſtood that this, and the five ſucceeding witneſſes, were to be called back, and re-examined, at the inſtance
of the paanel; but their exculpatory evidence was ultimately
diſpenſed with.

suspected it to be on his account that Miss Kinloch had sent for me. What conversation had you with Miss Kinloch? She told me that he appeared in a strange situation; that he had come there on the Sunday, with the buckles or strings out of his shoes. What did you say? I told her that, from the observations I had made myself, I concluded him perfectly mad, and that he should not be allowed to go about. What were the circumstances that made you think so? From the appearance of his eye, and the agitation in which he seemed to be. Has it been common for you to attend mad persons? No. What farther passed? I went down stairs to try to stop him from going away. I told him, if he would wait till I got some little refreshment, I would go with him to Haddington. This was the argument I made use of to induce him to come out of the chaise. What did he to say this? That he could not stop, as he would be too late for dinner at Edinburgh; and he accordingly ordered the postilion to drive on, and drove away.

After this, had you any further conversation with Miss Kinloch? Yes. I urged the propriety and necessity of confining him. I told Sir Francis the same thing that I had told Miss Kinloch; and he expressed a desire, that I might follow the Major to Edinburgh, and take the advice of the two Doctors Homes as to what should be done. Did you return to Haddington that night? Yes. And, when I returned there, I received a message from Mr Alexander Kinloch and Mr M‘Millan, who were at Mrs Fairbairn's, desiring me to go there. I went there, and saw Mr Alexander and Mr M‘Millan, and told them what had passed at Gilmerton. They told me, that they had met the Major going to Edinburgh. After dinner, Mr M‘Millan observed the chaise in which the Major was. It was driving as if he had been coming from Edinburgh. We looked to see which way the chaise would go, and it stopped at my shop door. I went down, and asked him to come up to Fairbairn's. He agreed to come. He shook hands with his brother Alexander, saying, he was very ill, and would never be better. He then walked about the room in
great

great agitation, and fhaking his head ; and he afterwards-
left the room. Did his brother or any body afk him to
ftay? We all afked him to ftay and take fome dinner, and
either go to Edinburgh, or return to Gilmerton. What
did he fay? He tried to eat and could not, and he fometimes fat on the forefide of a bed, which happened to
be in the room, but would not lie down. Did he afterwards agree to go to Gilmerton? Yes. I went in one
chaife with him, and Mr Mc Millan and Mr Alexander
went in another On our way, the pannel defired to get
out of the chaife. Did he give no reafon? No. Did he
return? No. I defired one of the poftilions to go after
him. He faid he would not return, becaufe he was going
back to Haddington. What was done then? We went
on to Gilmerton. About what time did you arrive
there? Between nine and ten. Did you ftay all night?
Yes. Were Sir Francis and Mifs Kinloch there? Yes.
How long did you ftay at Gilmerton? I ftaid all night, and
returned next morning.

Did you receive any meffage from Gilmerton the next
day, being Tuefday the 14th of April? Yes. I received
a card from Mr McMillan, informing me that the Major
had arrived, and defiring me to come down, and bring
what was neceffary. What did you underftand by this?
I underftood, that it was meant to confine the Major, and
that I fhould bring a ftrait waift-coat. I accordingly fet
out, and carried with me a ftrait waift-coat, and fent for
a nurfe, who fometimes attends deranged people. And
you went to Gilmerton with the nurfe? Yes, and I arrived there about 10 o'clock at night. After your arrival, did you take any meafures? I went to the Major,
and found him pretty quiet in his bed room, but ftill with
the fame wild look as the day before. Had you any converfation with Sir Francis, or any of the family, after
you came? Yes. Did you tell them, that you had brought
the waift-coat. I certainly would. They agreed in the
propriety of fecuring him. What was your reafon for
not fecuring him? I fpoke to the fervants frequently,
the

the butler, Mifs Kinloch's fervant, &c. but the moft of
them were either averfe, or afraid to do it. Do you
know what made them afraid to do it? No. Had you obferved arms about the Major? No, not then.

You fupped at Gilmerton. Did you fee the Major?
He came down to the parlour about three in the morning. He came down twice. When he came in for the
firft time, he walked about diftractedly, and complained of a violent pain in his bowels. Had you any
more converfation about the pain in his bowels? He
blamed, as the caufe, a dofe of pills which Sir Francis had
given him, and which, as the witnefs underftood from Sir
Francis, were analeptic pills. This was the firft time, he
fpoke of them? Yes. He faid thefe pills had done him
a great deal of ill, and he believed he was poifoned by
them. I advifed him to go to bed; upon which he left
the room. Did you go up to his bed-room? No. Did
he come down again? Yes. When? Soon after; within a very few minutes. Had you any converfation on
that occafion? No.

Lord Advocate. After you came with the ftrait waift-
coat, did you fee the Major at any time out of his own
room, before he came down to the parlour? I faw him
once, and fpoke to him. I faid he had much better not
go down in the fituation he then was in, for that Mifs
Kinloch was not gone to bed. This was between one
and two o'clock of Wednefday morning; and the Major
had no cloaths on, excepting his breeches and fhirt.

Solicitor General. Tell us all that paffed —*Witnefs,* I
faid to him, do not go down in that fituation. He faid he
would go down, for he wanted to fee Frank. I took hold
of him by the arm, and faid foftly, " Dear Sir, do not go
down in that fituation." When I took hold of him by
the arm, he drew a piftol. I let go his arm. He faid,
take care of yourfelf. At that very time, Sir Francis
was coming up ftairs. Sir Francis faid, " Gordon, what
is the matter?" He replied, " I do not know what to do.
Oh! I am ill, I cannot fleep." Did you or Sir Francis

fay

fay any thing to this? The Major went into his room; I
believe Sir Francis went into him. I went down ſtairs
ſoon after.

Solicitor General. You have told us that he came
down twice?— *Witneſs,* Yes. This was before the firſt
time. Tell us what happened the ſecond time? He came
down in the very ſame diſtracted manner: He walked up
and down: nobody ſpoke to him. Sir Francis went out
after him, then Alexander, and then I followed. Had
he all his clothes on when he came into the parlour? I
do not remember. He generally had one or both his hands
in his breeches pockets. The piſtol that I had ſeen, made
me ſuſpect, that he had his hands in his breeches pockets
holding piſtols. From what part of his clothes did he produce the piſtol when you ſaw it firſt? From his breeches
pocket. When I followed them as mentioned before, and
had come without the parlour door, I ſaw the flaſh of a
piſtol. I was then between the parlour door and the
trance. The flaſh was in the ſtair. Where was the pannel, and where was Sir Francis at this time? After ſeeing the flaſh, I was ſo confuſed, that I cannot recollect; but
I heard Sir Frnacis cry he was done for. I ran up to them.
They were ſtanding in the ſtair. Whether I aſſiſted in
ſecuring the pannel, I do not remember; but I aſſiſted
Sir Francis in going up ſtairs. After Sir Francis was
carried up ſtairs, what did you ſee? I ſaw a wound about
three or four inches below the breaſt-bone. When he
was laid in bed, I dreſſed the wound. Did you apprehend it to be mortal? Yes. Did you or Sir Francis ſay
any thing during the time you were with him? He ſaid it
was madneſs in him to attempt ſecuring his brother. I ſaid,
certainly it was. Was there any other aſſiſtance ſent
for? Yes, Dr Monro, Mr Bell, and my brother. When
did Sir Francis die? He died on the Thurſday evening,
about 11 o'clock. Are you ſatisfied that the wound was
the cauſe of his death; I am ſatisfied it was Did you examine the body along with the other gentlemen? Yes. Did
you find the bullet? I was preſent when it was extracted.
Mr Bell extracted it, while Sir Francis was alive. The
witneſs

witnefs was fhewn a certificate of what had been obferved in opening the body of Sir Francis after his death, and was afked if he had figned this certificate? to which queftion he anfwered in the affirmative.

Did you fee the pannel again, or had you any converfation with him, after you went up with Sir Francis? I do not remember of feeing him till he was in Haddington Jail. After the piftol was fired, I remember nothing about him. When did you fee him? I faw him in Haddington Jail, on Friday the 16th of April. What converfation paffed there? I had no particular converfation. I went up with Dr. Home, and Mr Goldie the minifter of the parifh. Mr Goldie faid, that as his brother was now dead, it fell to him to give directions as to what was to be done at Gilmerton; for, though he was accufed of a moft horrid crime, yet he was not yet indicted, nor tried by the laws of his country. He replied, that he was in fuch a ftate of mind, that he could give no directions or advice about any thing. The next thing that Mr Goldie faid was, that it was the opinion of lawyers, that he might, in the prefence of witneffes, appoint Mr Frafer and him to act for him. What anfwer did the Major make? I do not remember the anfwer; but he agreed to it. You faid the Major appeared in great horror: What did he fay? He faid, it was a fatal day. Afterwards, Dr. Home afked him, If he would wifh to fee Major Mackay and Dr. Farquharfon. He faid, he would be very glad to fee them.

Lord Advocate. When Sir Francis left the parlour, immediately before the accident, did you know for what purpofe he went? No. What was your purpofe? Sir Francis and I agreed as to the propriety of fecuring the Major, if he came in a fecond time; but I did not leave the room with the intention of fecuring him. Did you fend for any of the out fervants to affift in feizing him? I know they were fent for. Did you know that they were difmiffed? No. I did not fee any of them at the time the accident happened. When did you fee any of them?

them? I faw them between twelve and two o'clock. I do not know that they were fent home.

Lord Juftice Clerk. The laft time you faw the pannel, previous to the event that took place, Is it your opinion, that he was then in fuch a fituation, as not to diftinguifh moral good from evil, and not to know that murder was a crime? I cannot fay. I do not know what he could diftinguifh. Is it your opinion? When I faw him on the Monday, and on the Tuefday, I confidered him mad.

Solicitor General. Was he mad to fuch a degree, as not to be able to diftinguifh good from evil? I cannot anfwer the queftion in any other way than that I thought him perfectly mad.

The witnefs was ordered to withdraw.

Mr Hope. I could have wifhed, that a queftion of this nature had been allowed to come from the profecutor, becaufe then I might have commented upon it with greater freedom than I can do, fince it has been fuggefted by the Court. The queftion, however, I think, was a proper one; and it was properly anfwered. The witnefs, after repeated interrogations, faid, That he could not take upon him to tell what the pannel could diftinguifh; but that when he (the witnefs) faw him on the Monday, and on the Tuefday, he confidered him mad. He fays again, " I cannot anfwer the queftion otherwife, than " that I thought him *perfectly mad.*" And I muft fay, that, as a profeffional man, he could not anfwer it otherwife than he has done. My Lords, I am not of the witnefs's profeffion; but, as a man who has paid fome attention to the human mind, and to human nature, I muft repeat, that the queftion was anfwered as it ought to have been.

My Lords, I have made fome obfervations on madmen myfelf. Perfons in that unhappy fituation are too often expofed to the impertinent vifits of ftrangers; at leaft, it ufed to be fo in London: and well I remember, when at an early period of life, led by the idle curiofity of a boy, I have gone to view the places of their confinement. But,

my

my Lords, I hardly ever faw a man fo mad, (though lying naked, and chained, on ftraw,) who, if the abftract queftion were put,—Do you think murder a crime?—would not anfwer in the affirmative. Madmen, my Lords, will often talk rationally on any fubject, until you come across that particular topic, which has deranged their underftanding. I therefore fubmit, that it is not proper to prefs the witnefs for a more particular anfwer. Has he not faid, that the pannel was *perfectly* mad? The profecutor talks of *degrees* of madnefs, but there is no degree in *perfect* madnefs? this is already the fuperlative degree. And when the witnefs, a profeffional man, has declared, that he cannot anfwer the queftion otherwife, I fay, that any other anfwer which he may give, cannot be an anfwer according to his confcience.

My Lords, had not the witnefs been a profeffional man, I fhould not have infifted fo much upon the point; but as a man who, from his profeffion, muft know fomething of the nature of this difeafe, I do repeat, he could not have anfwered the queftion in any other manner; and I do fubmit, that he cannot be forced to give any other anfwer than that which he has already given.

Lord Advocate. My Lords, I do not intend to prefs the witnefs any farther on that point. If my brother fuppofes that I meant to prefs him to make an anfwer contrary to his confcience,—that I meant to pufh him to give me a different anfwer from that which he has chofen to give,—he has much miftaken my meaning. When I proceeded to prefs him a little farther, it was only to difcover what was meant under the words " perfectly mad." What I mean to, prefs from him goes thus far, to fee whether the fame general queftion, at any particular period of time, will receive the fame anfwer. This I contend, I am entitled to do; and I fhall judge from the anfwers that may be given, what inference I fhall draw to the Jury.

The witnefs was recalled.

Lord Advocate. When you faw the pannel at Mrs
Fair-

Fairbairn's on the Monday, was he in such a situation as to discern good from evil, or to know that murder was a crime? I cannot say that he could not.

When you saw him next night in his own room at Gilmerton, down to the time of his appearance in the parlour, can you say, during that period, from ten at night to three in the morning, that the pannel was in a condition to discern good from evil, or to know that murder was a crime? I have not had much practice in cases of insanity; and what such persons may think, I am at a loss to say.

You have told us, that you cannot say, that, when at Fairbairn's, the pannel could not discern good from evil; and that, with regard to the second period, you have not had much practice in cases of lunacy,—very proper answers. Now, did you observe any difference in that time, and on what side lay the difference? I did not observe any difference until he came into the parlour, when he appeared worse.

Mr GEORGE SOMNER *cross examined by* Mr HUME.—Deponed, That when at Haddington, the pannel was restless, agitated, and unhappy,—could not eat,—trembled so as to need assistance in carrying a tumbler of wine and water to his head ;—did not seem disposed to drink, and got no spirits there that he knows of : That the motion of returning to Gilmerton, was not the pannel's own thought, but the witness's motion.

Mr Hume. If you were carried from this room to bedlam, and there shown a lunatic in his cell; if this lunatic, on being asked, *If murder is a crime?* should answer, *Yes,* would you, on the faith of that answer, think it safe to put yourself in his power, or to venture within his reach ?

Mr Somner.—I would not.

Mr Hume. May not a person be mad, and yet know his keeper or others who are much about him, and be liable to be intimidated and controuled by them.

Mr Somner. I think he may.

Mr

Mr Hume. Do you think that the pannel, on the Tuesday evening, when he came to the parlour, was in such a situation of mind as to be capable of distinguishing the good or evil intentions of those who came near him, or interfered with him? or, to be more particular, Do you think he was able to distinguish, and be thankful for the good intention of a medical person like yourself, who attended to serve and assist him, from the intention of an enemy, who should come to harm him.

Mr Somner. I do not think he could.

Mr Hume. If you had attempted to wrest the pistol from him at the top of the stair, would you have run a risk of your life?

Mr Somner. I think I would.

Mr Hume. If you had tried to seize him when Sir Francis did, or if you had been in the same position as Sir Francis was with respect to him, at the time when the pistol was fired, do you believe that you would have met with the same fate?

Mr Somner. I believe I would.

Mr Hume. Did it appear to you, that the pannel, when Sir Francis was with him, was soothed and pleased with his kindness.

Mr Somner. It did rather appear to me, that he was more quiet when Sir Francis was with him than at other times.

Mr Hume. Was he ever alone with Sir Francis in the course of the Tuesday evening.

Mr Somner. I did understand that the pannel and Sir Francis were at times in the pannel's bed-room by themselves, but I cannot positively say so from my own knowledge?

Mr Hume. In the course of the Tuesday evening, were the pannel's conduct and appearance such as to persuade you, that the advice which you had given, to have him secured and confined, was a wrong, or groundless, or unnecessary advice?

Mr Somner. No, I still thought it right.

Mr

Mr Hume. At the time when the pannel fired the piftol, was he fully dreffed, fo as to be in a condition to make his efcape if he had been fo difpofed?

Mr Somner. He was not.

Lord Swinton. You fay you brought a woman and a ftrait waift-coat? Does it confift with your knowledge, that the pannel was informed of this? I do not think he was informed of the waift-coat, but he knew of the nurfe.

Lord Advocate. I have afked you already your opinion of his fanity on the Monday and Tuefday. I put the fame queftion again. When you faw him in jail, did you then think him capable of difcerning good from evil, and of knowing that murder was a crime? I thought him then fenfible.

Mr Moncrieff, (one of the Jury.) How long have you been furgeon to the family of Gilmerton? Twelve years. Do you know of any hereditary difeafes in the family? No. Can you affign any caufe for the pannel's derangement? No. Do you know whether the pannel, at any time previous to the accident, endured a remarkable degree of cold? I do not know. Do you know whether he refifted the taking of food? I mentioned that he would eat nothing on the Monday. Do you know whether he ufed to fleep well? I have obferved that he was very reftlefs.

Do you think that the refiftance of cold, hunger and fleep, affords the beft marks of diftinguifhing infanity, from cafes where it is only feigned to ferve a particular purpofe? I think it does.

Mr M'Aulay, (another of the Jury.) When you faw the pannel in the chaife, did he do any thing, or fay any thing outrageous? No. Did you think him drunk? No. Do you think that drink might have produced the fame behaviour? I never faw him in the fame fituation before. Do not you think that the paffions of the mind, fuch as fear, anger, revenge, jealoufy, &c. may produce temporary fits of infanity? I think they might have put a perfon much in the fame fituation,

GEORGE

GEORGE DOUGLAS, *examined by* Mr BURNET.——
Were you a servant to Miss Kinloch in April laſt? Yes.
Do you remember any accident that happened about the
15th of that month? Yes. It happened between three and
four in the morning. What accident do you allude to?
I was in the butler's parlour.——I heard the report of
a piſtol. Where did you go when you heard the report? I ran into the dining room, and laid hands upon
Major Gordon. Did you not ſee Sir Francis before
you went into the dining room? I juſt got a glance of him
in paſſing. Did you ſee any piſtols? I lifted a piſtol
within the dining room door. Was it loaded? No. It
was empty, but appeared to have been newly diſ-
charged. Did you not ſee another piſtol? I received
another from the poſtilion, which he ſaid he had found on
Major Gordon. Was it loaded? Yes. I afterwards ſaw
it drawn. (Here the witneſs was ſhewn a pair of piſtols.)
Are theſe the piſtols you ſaw? Yes they are.

What did you do with Major Gordon? We laid him
on the carpet, and held him down, until a woman came
and put a handkerchief on his face. He then had a ſtrait
waiſt-coat put upon him, and was taken up to his own
room. What did he ſay to you? He cried to let him
live for one hour, and he would give us L. 100 a piece.
Did he ſpeak of what he had done? He aſked if his brother
was dead. Do you remember any thing more? After he
was bound, he aſked what we were going to do with him,
if we were going to cut his throat, or ſtab him. Was he
carried up to his room? He walked up. What paſſed
then? He ſaid, " I have done an awful thing?" Any
more? I went away. When did you ſee him again?
Sometime through the day. What ſituation was he in?
Did you hear him ſay any thing? He lay very quiet in
his bed.

Did the pannel deſire to ſee any perſon in particular?
He aſked how his ſiſter was, and wanted to ſee Mr Fraſer, but Mr Fraſer would not go near him. He aſked
alſo how his brother Sir Francis was. Did you, or any
body

body, mention in what situation he was? When he afked, I faid he was very poorly. Did he underftand the anfwer that was made? He feemed to be forry. How long was he in that situation? Till Wednesday night.

When he was conveyed to Haddington Jail, who went with him? Mr Hay Smith, writer, from Haddington, accompained him in the carriage.

Did he fay he was forry for what he had done? No; but he feemed to be forry, and sometimes appeared not to underftand what was faid.

GEORGE DOUGLAS, *crofs examined by* Mr HUME.— Deponed, That the pannel, after being feized, faid to Sir Francis's fervant, *that his mafter had poifoned him, and that otherwife he would not have done to him what he did:* That the pannel, at the time of doing the deed, was in no condition to make his efcape, having nothing on but his breeches and a great coat.

ALEXANDER CAMPBELL, *examined by* Mr BURNET.— Were you a fervant at Gilmerton laft April? Yes, I was poftilion. Do you remember Sir Francis being wounded? Yes. At what period of the month did it happen? I do not remember the day: it was about the middle of the month. Tell us what paffed? I was in the Butler's parlour, and heard the report of a piftol between three and four in the morning, and went into the dining-room, where I faw Major Gordon, and two or three fervants. Did you fee Sir Francis after you heard the report of the piftol? No. Did you fee any piftols? Yes, I faw one in the hands of one of the lads. Did you take any piftols from the prifoner? Yes, I took one from his pocket. What pocket? He had on a great coat and breeches.—The piftol was taken out of his breeches pocket. Was it loaded? I believe it was, but cannot fay for certain, as I gave it to one of the fervants. (Here the witnefs was fhewn a piftol.) Do you know that piftol? Yes. It is one of them I faw.

What

What was done with the Major after the piftols were taken from him? There was a jacket put on him. Was he taken to his room? Yes. What did he fay? He faid that he had been poifoned by his elder brother; and that he knew he would have been feized, whether he had fhot Sir Francis or not. What more? He faid that he would give them L.100 a-piece to let him live one hour. What farther converfation paffed in the bed-room? Nothing more. Did you fee him carried away? Yes, the fame night. Who went with him? Mr Smith from Haddington.

Juryman. Did the Major offer to ftrike you, when you feized him? No; he fuffered us quietly to put on the jacket.

ALEXANDER CAMPBELL, *crofs interrogated by* Mr HUME. —Deponed, that, when the piftol was fired, the pannel had on a great coat, breeches, fhirt, and ftockings, but was without his waiftcoat, and he thinks had nothing on his feet: That he certainly had not fhoes on; and, if he had any thing on, it was only flippers.

WALTER GIBSON, *examined by* Mr BURNET.— Were you fervant to Sir Francis Kinloch? Yes. Do you remember of Sir Francis being wounded in April laft? Yes. Do you remember at what time it happened? It was about three of a Wednefday morning. I was in the butler's parlour, and heard the piftol difcharged. Did you affift in feizing the Major? Yes. I took a piftol from his pocket. Was it loaded? I believe fo. What paffed when you bound the Major? He fpoke a good deal while we were binding him. He called out, that he had been poifoned by his brother. Did he fay any thing befides? He cried to let him alone, as he would live but one hour. Any thing more? I do not recollect. What did you do with him after he was bound? He was carried to bed.

WALTER GIBSON, *crofs examined by* Mr HUME.— Deponed, That the pannel, when he fired the piftol, was

not

not in condition to efcape or leave the houfe, being without his fhoes, and as he thinks without fome of his clothes:
That Sir Francis, on being told that the pannel was fecured
faid, *Poor unhappy man.* And that Sir Francis, on the Wednefday evening, on being told that the Major was carried
to Haddington, faid, " *What are they going to do with him*
" *there. Why dont they carry him to Edinburgh?*" but whether he meant to a goal or a madhoufe he did not explain.

ALEXANDER MENIE, *examined by* Mr BURNET.————
You were butler to the late Sir Francis Kinloch? Yes.
You know that he was wounded in April laft? Yes.
Were you in his bed-room after he received the wound?
Yes. When there, Did Sir Francis fay any thing about
the wound, or the perfon that had given it him? No.
How long did you remain in the room? About three
quarters of an hour. Were you frequently with him before he died? Yes. On thefe occafions, did you hear him
fay any thing about the pannel? No. Did you fee the
pannel during this time? No. I did not fee him till a fortnight after.

Lord Advocate. How long have you been in this fami-
ily? Nine years. Did you ever, during thefe nine years,
hear any of the family fay, that the pannel was infane?
I overheard old Sir David fay to a gentleman, that Gordon was juft going mad again. Was the pannel in the
houfe at the time? He was ftaying at Gilmerton, but was
from home on a vifit. Did you obferve any appearances
of madnefs about him yourfelf? I obferved him unfettled.
Were any fteps, or any advice taken in the family about
him? Not fo far as I know. Did he continue to come
about the houfe, and to be inthe fame way as formerly?
Yes.

HAY SMITH, *writer in Haddington, examined by* Mr
BURNET.——
Do you remember being in the houfe of Gilmerton on the
Wednefday night after Sir Francis was wounded? Yes.

E   Had

Had you occasion to see the Major? Yes. What was
the occasion of your going there? I went as a messenger
to take him to Haddington Jail. Who accompanied the
Major and you to Haddington? A servant.

Lord Advocate. Do you remember any thing that passed while on the road? The Major was in great distress,
but said nothing. Did any thing pass when you got to
Haddington Jail? I put him into a small apartment, and
went to inform the Provost, who ordered a better apartment. When you first saw him, Who was with him? I
went up with Mr Goldie the minister. Did the pannel
hold any conversation with you? He conversed with the
minister. Did the answers, which he made to Mr Goldie,
appear to you collected and rational? Yes. Do you recollect any particular topic? Not, when I was first in his
room. At the time I went up to take him away, which
was about eight in the evening, he asked me as a lawyer,
to take a protest against these proceedings, and then appeared very confused. Did you see him again? Yes, in
Haddington Jail. How long did he remain there? Three
or four days. Did he upon those occasions, when you saw
him there, return rational answers? He did. Did you
accompany him to Edinburgh? Yes. What conversation passed? About the weather. Was he rational?
Yes.

BENJAMIN BELL, *Surgeon in Edinburgh, examined by Mr*
BURNET.

Were you sent for to Gilmerton on the 15th of April
last? I was. Were you informed of the purpose for which
you were called? I was informed at Gilmerton of the business. I was told that Sir Francis was shot that morning.

Lord Advocate. What passed when you saw Sir Francis? I found him lying in his bed in great distress. He
had been shot under the breast-bone. Did you believe
the wound to be mortal? From all the symptoms, I judged him to be a dying man. Did you remain in the house
till Sir Francis died? No, I waited till six o'clock next
morning,

morning, not thinking it neceffary to remain longer. Are
you of opinion, that the wound was the caufe of his death?
Yes.

Did Sir Francis hold any converfation with you concerning the perfon who wounded him? He never did;
except afking what was become of that *unhappy m n.*—
Did he not name the perfon? No. Did Dr Monro attend? Dr Monro was fent for along with me, but did not
go. When you firft of all examined the wound, on Wednefday morning, did Sir Francis tell you how he had got
it? I had been told, that the perfon who fired the piftol was
uppermoft in the ftair, and therefore, I imagined the ball
might have taken an oblique direction; but Sir Francis
gave me a diftinct account of the accident, by which I
underftood, that the ball had gone right acrofs his body;
and I felt it with my hand near the back bone, from
whence it was extracted. Did you open the body after
death? Yes, in company with Meff. Somners. There
was a report drawn up. Would you know the report
again? Yes. (Here the report of what had been remarked on opening the body of Sir Francis, was fhewn to,
and recognifed by Mr Bell.)

How did Sir Francis defcribe the fituation of the perfon who fhot him? He faid, he was ftanding on the fame
ftep of the ftair with himfelf, and that the piftol almoft
touched his body; and this account tallied exactly with
the fituation in which I found the ball.

Lord Juftice Clerk. Did he name the perfon? No, he
never named him.

(Here the witnefs was fhewn the ball which he had extracted from the body of Sir Francis Kinloch. It was
wrapped in a piece of paper, upon which Mr Bell had
marked the initial letters of his name.)

Lord Advocate. Did you know the family of Gilmerton before this accident? Yes. I fometimes attended the
late Sir David. When you went to Gilmerton on thefe
occafions,

occafions, did you fee the pannel? Yes. Did you ever know, or underftand that the prifoner was infane? I never did.

Had you occafion to attend the pannel fince the 24th of May? Yes. At Mr Warrender's defire, I have attended him in Edinburgh Jail fince that time, twice a-week. Now, I afk you this as a profeffional man, Did you ever fee, believe, or judge him to be under any degree of infanity?. I never did. He always behaved with propriety; but he appeared under great anxiety of mind, and depreffion of fpirits. Did he feem to know his fituation? Yes.

Mr BENJAMIN BELL, *crofs examined by* Mr HUME.— Deponed, That he vifited the pannel twice a-week, from the 24th May,—and fometimes remained with him from 15 to 20 minutes: That he generally fent up previous notice of his being there: That he cannot give an opinion upon thefe his vifits, that the pannel might not be furious on the 15th of April,—nor ever that he might not fhow fymptons of derangement in the intervals of his vifits;—for that the ftate of infane perfons is liable to fudden and unaccountable variations: That he could not pretend to know a madman by the ftate of his pulfe, or the feeling of his fkin; for that, though, in the beginning of infanity, there is often fever, yet a confirmed ftate of infanity is not ordinarily attended with any; and that, in this, the delirium of a fever is diftinguifhed from that of infanity: That madmen very often can diftinguifh their keeper, or others who are much about them: That in many inftances, they are capable of diffimulation, and fhow cunning and contrivance to gain their ends: That one of the moft conftant fymptoms of madnefs, is a jealoufy of plots and confpiracies againft them; and that moft frequently the objects of thefe fufpicions are their beft friends, or the perfons to whom they had been moft attached: That the moft certain means of diftinguifhing a madman, are 1ft, By his actions and conduct; and,
2dly,

2*dly*, By the appearance of his countenance, especially of his eye, which has a peculiar wildness: That restless-ness,—want of sleep,—odd postures,—strange gestures,—and the like, are also among the indications of the malady: That if a person has been subject to occasional derangement, and should swallow a great quantity of laudanum, this, in his case, might be more apt to produce a furiosity of a few days, and the person afterwards make a quick recovery, than in the case of a person who had never been subject to such disorder: That the confinement, solitude, and quiet of a jail, would be likely means to promote and assist such recovery.

Dr. ALEXANDER MONRO, *Physician in Edinburgh, examined by* Mr BURNET.——
Have you attended the pannel in Jail? Yes. How often have you visited him? four different times since the 24th of May. What situation did you usually find him in with regard to his mind? I saw no marks of insanity. Did you converse with him? I did. Did you feel his pulse when you visited him? Always, and I found it calm and regular.

Dr. MONRO, *cross examined by* Mr HUME.——
Deponed, That he had paid the pannel four visits in Jail after the 24th May. Being asked the same questions as Mr Bell, he made the same answers in substance; and in particular, being asked, whether madmen were more apt to be jealous of their enemies or of their friends and near connections? He answered, That their friends were most commonly the objects of their suspicion, and that he thought it natural it should be so; for as madmen were not sensible of their own condition, or of the necessity of restraining them, and as friends and relations were chiefly active in controuling or imposing restraints on them, so these persons irritated them, and in consequence became the objects of resentment. He added, that in his visits to the pannel, which might be from 7 to 15 minutes,

he

he avoided any topic that could irritate him ; and that if
he had remained a whole, or half a day with him, he could
better have judged of his condition : And, upon the
whole, That he could only give an opinion as relative to
the times and occasions when he saw him, and nothing
more.

Lord Advocate. Did you ever, in the course of your
practice, know a person who went mad for forty-eight hours,
and then recovered and continued well? Never, except
when the person had swallowed a great quantity of liquor,
or owing to some adventitious cause.

Mr Hope. May not a person, who has been subject to
fits of madness, become suddenly infane, and recover
again? He is more apt to do so, than a person who never
was infane. May not the taking of laudanum, by a person
who has been occasionally infane, produce a fit of infanity? Yes.

CHARLES HAY, *Esq, Advocate, examined by the Solicitor-
General.—*
Were you well accquainted with the late Sir Francis
Kinloch? I certainly was

Did he confult you upon any points after his father's
death? He did afk my opinion refpecting his father's fettlements sometimes after his death.

Will you be fo good as mention every thing which you
remember that paffed between Sir Francis and you upon
that occasion ; and, in particular, any thing refpecting differences which had occurred between him and the pannel.

Mr Hay, (addreffing the Court.) My Lord, it is a delicate fituation in which I ftand, I am called upon to give evidence, not to facts confiftent with my perfonal knowledge,
but to difclofe conversations of a confidential and private
nature, that paffed between Sir Francis Kinloch and me,
not only as a friend, but in my profeffional character of a
lawyer. I fhould therefore be glad to know from the
Court,

Court, whether it is their opinion, that I am bound to give an account of thefe confidential converfations.

Lord Juftice Clerk. Your delicacy, Mr Hay, is proper; but it is the opinion of the Court, you ought to anfwer the queftion. When called upon in fuch circumftances, and in a cafe of this importance, it is your duty to give the Court and Jury all the information in your power.

Mr Hay. From the regard I bore to Sir Francis Kinloch, I intended to go cut to Gilmerton the very day after the laft Winter Seffion rofe, in order to pay my refpects to him on occafion of his father Sir David Kinloch's death; but, being unwilling to put him under any reftraint, I wrote to Mr Duncan M'Millan, who, I knew, was then at Gilmerton, rather than to Sir Francis himfelf, and defired him to let me know, whether it would be perfectly convenient for Sir Francis to receive my vifit at that time. Mr M'Millan returned me an anfwer, that Sir Francis would be in Edinburgh before the time I propofed to be at Gilmerton, and that I would fee him. Sir Francis arrived in town upon the 10th or 11th of March, and dined with me on the 12th or 13th, when he took occafion to mention, that his reafon for coming to town, was to advife with his friends concerning differences which had arifen betwixt him and fome of the other branches of the family, concerning his father's fettlements, or rather after incidents.

Mr Burnet. Explain what were thefe after incidents, and with what branches of the family thefe differences had happened.

Mr Hay. Sir Francis told me, that after Sir David's fettlements were opened, appointing him his father's fgeneral diponee, he, having got the key of the repofitory in which Sir David lodged his papers, obferved, that Sir David had been accuftomed to preferve almoft every letter that he received, on matters of trivial importance, and other papers of no confequence, for which reafon, he he defired Mr M'Millan, and Mr Frazer, fheriff-clerk of Haddington, to feparate the rubbifh from the material papers, and to deftroy the former, which he underftood that they accordingly burned, or at leaft great part of it. This infpired a jealoufy into the mind of his brother the Major, that papers were deftroyed to the prejudice of the younger branches of the family, which he communicated to his younger brother Mr Alexander; and it was on account of this mifunderftanding, that Sir Francis told me, he had come to town to take my opinion and that of Mr Solicitor-General on the fubject.— Sir Francis then fhewed me the general difpofition by his father in his favour; and, on reading it, I told him I was clearly of opinion, it was properly conceived, fo that it was impoffible there could be room for any difpute between him and his brothers, unlefs it fhould fo happen, that the claim of legitim to the younger children was not difcharged in their father's and mother's contract of marriage, in confideration of fpecial provifions being fettled on them, which I mentioned to him would probably be the cafe, as few contracts of marriage were entered into, at the fight of regular men of bufinefs, without a claufe to that purpofe. I having then explained to Sir Francis the nature and extent of the claim ot legitim which would ly in this particular cafe, he immediately faid, that the provifions fettled by Sir David on the younger children, were fuperior to what they could claim in virtue of the legitim, even if it were not difcharged; whereupon I expreffed my fatisfaction, that there could be no ground for any legal difpute, and it was fuggefted that there would be no neceffity to trouble the Solicitor-General for any opinion on the cafe, at leaft till Sir Francis fhould have an opportunity of looking into his father's marriage-contract, which he was not then poffeffed of. A great deal of converfation paffed upon the fubject, with the exact particulars of which I cannot now charge my memory, but I am certain I have told the import of it.

Had

H *d* you any fubfequent converfation with Sir F*r*anci*s*
on this fubject?

I called upon Sir Francis a few days thereafter at Dumbreck's hotel, where he was confined with a heavy cold.
He then defired that I would give him a written opinion
upon the fubject of which we had formerly converfed, to be
communicated to his brothers. I declined giving him a
formal opinion, mentioning, that it occured to me, that a
letter written, as from one friend to another, might have
a better effect. Sir Francis agreed with me, and I accordingly wrote, and delivered to him out of my own
hand, a letter containing my fentiments.

Mr Hay, *crofs interrogated by Mr* Hume.—
Did Sir Francis afterwards mention to you, that he had
communicated your letter to his brothers?

In eight or ten days thereafter, I was with Sir Francis
in a mixed company, and In a whifper afked him, Whether
he had fhewn my letter to his brother? To which he anfwered in general terms, that he had; but no farther
converfation paffed, and I never faw him afterwards fo far
as I recollect, as this was either the Saturday fe'ennight,
or Saturday fortnight preceding his deceafe.

Did Sir Francis write to you, complaining that your letter had not had the defired effect?

No, he never did.

Lird Juftice Clrek. Did you underftand that the difference between Sir Francis and the pannel had rifen to a
great height.

To a very great height indeed.

The Reverend Mr George Goldie, *Minifter of the Gof-*
pel at Atheljtoneford, examined by Mr. Burner.——
Had you occafion to go to the houfe of Gilmerton foon after Sir Francis was wounded? Yes, I went there on the
morning after the accident happened; I heard of it between eight and nine, and immediately went down. Did
you fee the Major? Yes. What paffed? After I had been

F   fome

some time in the house, I was made to understand, that
Major Gordon wanted to see me.. I accordingly went up,
and found him lying bound in bed with a strait waist-coat
on, and in a very distracted state. I asked him how he was;
he answered " very ill." He then asked me to sit down
by his bed-side. I did so, and asked him if he recollected
what had passed? he said he did. I asked him, If he was
not filled with horror at what he had done? He answered with a furious air, and in a low tone of voice uncommonly stern, " No." my own feelings were much distressed,
and I exclaimed " Are you not filled with horror at the
" recollection of a deed that has destroyed one of the wor-
" thiest of men, and best of brothers,—a deed, that has
" thrown a family into a state of distraction, and a whole
" country into the most extreme misery?" He again answered in the same tone, that what he had done was in self defence. " There was," (said he) " a deliberate plan to form-
" ed to destroy me." " Who told you of that plan?" He replied, " that he knew it well." " You could know it only
(said I,) " from the jealousy, or suspicion of your own
" mind, for the worthy man, whom you have destroyed, was
" incapable of forming a plan against any human being."
" I shall die, (said he) this evening ; my brother has
" poisoned me. He has given me pills, which have al-
" ready deprived me of the use of all the lower parts of my
" body." I replied, I knew nothing about pills ; but, if he
had got pills, they had been given him with a view to do
him good, not to hurt him. Had you any further conversation? He cried, to take away the people that were about
him. I believe, he meant the woman, and the man servant who attended him, who, he thought had a design to
murder him; and he insisted upon me staying with him
upon that account. He said, he understood there was no
danger of Sir Francis. I answered, that whoever had
told him so, had been deceiving him ; for I had the best
authority, the authority of the medical gentlemen, for
saying, that the danger was most eminent, and that, in all
probability his brother would be be a corpse before evening.—

ing.—Did you fee him upon any occafion in the afternoon?
Yes. Towards the evening he became very outrageous,
and attempted to burft afunder his bonds. He cried,
that he wanted to fee me; and, when I went to him, he
infifted that I fhould ufe every endeavour to fet him at
liberty. He ordered the fervants to go out of the room;
for, he had fomething particular to fay to me. I defired
the fervants to walk out. He then told me, that he muft
be put in a chair before he could communicate what he had
to fay to me. I told him, he could inform me of any thing
very well where he was. He then told me, it was about
money matters: he faid, he had feveral hundred pounds
which no body knew of, and he wanted to fettle it. I
told him there were men of bufinefs in the houfe, who
might be confulted about that, and then fent to Mr Frafer and Mr Smith. When Mr Smith came into the
room, he faid to him, " who has a right to ufe me in this
" tyrannical manner; is it not competent to take a pro-
" teft againft them?" Mr Smith faid, it could not be
done. The Major then fpoke of fettling fome money
matters; and Mr Smith having faid, it would be better to
delay that bufinefs till afterwards, the Major replied,
" why not now,"
    " Procraftination is the thief of time."
    Had you occafion to fee him afterwards in Haddington
Jail? Yes. What converfation paffed there? I told him,
that I had come at the particular defire of the friends of
the family, to receive directions about the management
of affairs at Gilmerton. He declined giving any directions, but left the whole to his brother Sandie. I informed him, that his brother was from home, and that
the friends of the family were of opinion, that fome directions were abfolutely neceffary in the meantime. He
faid, that the friends ought to do what they thought moft
proper. I then told him, that the friends of the family
had fuggefted, that Mr Frafer and I fhould be appointed
to take the management, and that they wifhed to have
his confent; and that, if this propofal met with his ap-
probation,

probation, I would write out, in his name, and in prefence of two respectable witneffes, a power to this effect; to all which he agreed, adding, that he was in fuch a ftate, that he could not attend to any bufinefs. A power was accordingly written in prefence of Dr James Home and Mr George Somner, and a claufe fubjoined, that, if Mr Frafer and I fhould meet with any difficulties, we fhould take the advice of gentlemen of the law.

The Reverend Mr GEÓRGE GOLDIE, *crofs examined by* Mr HUMF.—

Do you recollect what converfations you have had with the pannel fince he came to Edinburgh? I have feen him frequently in Edinburgh, and occafionally mentioned to him how he had acted, and the fatal event that had taken place. His anfwers were various. At the times when he was correct, he expreffed great regret that he had not been feized and difarmed before he committed the unlucky deed. It was not merely regret, he expreffed horror at the deed, and aftonifhment, from what he had afterwards learned as to his fituation at the time, that it had not been put out of his power to do any thing of the kind. He blamed his friends in very ftrong terms, for having treated him with fo much lenity. Had you any converfation on the day of the accident, about an Englifh bank bill? Yes. In the courfe of that day, at Gilmerton, when Mr Hay Smith was prefent, and it was propofed to make an inventory of the pannel's money and papers. He was afked, If he had any money in his pockets? To which he anfwered, he had a bill for L.30 in them. Upon fearching, I told him, I could not find it. He faid, he was perfectly certain of having brought it to Gilmerton the day before. I then went down ftairs, and informed Mr Frafer of this circumftance. Mr Frafer faid, " we know " about the bill; he gave it to William Reid the gard- " ner laft night at Beanfton, who gave it to Sir Francis." I returned, and told we had found it, and in what manner.

He

He had no recollection of having done fo; and juſt ſaid, "Honeſt William."

Lord Advocate. How long have you been ſetiled at Athelſtoneford? Since April 1778. Is Gilmerton in the pariſh of Athelſtoneford? Yes. You would be ſometimes at Gilmerton? I had the honour to be frequently there. Of courſe, you would be acquainted with the family? I was well acquainted with all the family. Was the pannel at the bar frequently there during your viſits? He was. Did you ever, previous to his father's death, know that the pannel was inſane? Never, from my own perſonal knowledge or obſervation. Did you ever, previous to Sir David's death, hear that the family had taken any ſteps to confine him? I never heard of their taking any, previous to Sir David's death. Did you ever hear of the pannel being inſane? Yes. I remember in June 1790, I went to Dunbar, to aſſiſt a brother miniſter in diſpenſing the Sacrament. I lodged at Mr Lorimer's, who informed me, that he had ſeen my friend, Major Gordon, who had behaved in a very ſtrange manner: That he was very glad I had come, for, if he had not had the proſpect of ſeeing me, he would certainly have written to deſire me to inform the family; and he told me, that the behaviour of the Major was ſuch, that he conſidered him as deranged. Did he give you any reaſon for that opinion? He ſaid, that he put himſelf into ſtrange attitudes, and went about the room beating his breaſt and head: That he ordered a chaiſe for Gilmerton, but in place of going to Gilmerton, he drove through Dunbar, and, as Mr Lorimer was informed, had gone to Dunſe. Did you hear of any other inſtances? No. Did you inform any of the family of what Mr Lorimer had told you? I mentioned it to Sir Francis, who was then Mr Francis Kinloch. Since Sir David's death, did you make any obſervations on the pannel's behaviour? I have ſeen him in great depreſſion of ſpirits. Did you form an opinion, that he was inſane? The laſt time that I had the pleaſure of ſeeing him at Gilmerton, previous to the late melancholy

choly event, was on the 28th of March. An old coachman of
the family, (Peter Dickfon,) feeing the Major in a very
diftrefsed fituation, had confidered it his duty to call at
the Manfe the day before, when I was from home, and
faid, that he thought the Major fhould not be left by himfelf. On the morning after this information, I went to Gilmerton, and found the Major walking in the avenue. He
told me, that he did not know what was the matter with
him; he could not fettle in any one place, nor fix his mind
on any one fubject. I thought he was not fit to be left
by himfelf; and though I had occafion to leave him at
this time, and though he did not as ufual invite me back
to dinner, yet I returned, and found him walking about.
Fearing he might think I intruded, I felt myfelf obliged
to apologize. I faid, " You well think, Sir, your evil
" genius haunts you to day; but I thought you would be
" dull by yourfelf, and have therefore ufed the freedom
" to come to dine with you." He thanked me, and faid
he was very glad of my company. Did you obferve any
thing uncommon in his behaviour on any other occafion?
Yes. On the 12th of April, the Sunday immediately before Sir Francis's death, I faw a carriage ftop oppofite to
the manfe. I immediately went out, and faw the Major;
and, upon my afking him, he came out of the carriage.
When we came in, (we had juft done dinner,) I afked him if he had dined? and he faid he had; I faid that
it was much earlier than his ufual hour of dinner. Suppo-
fing that he faid he had dined, with a view not to give
trouble to the family, I told he could have a dinner immediately and without any trouble. He repeated, that he
had already dined. I then afked him, If he would take a
glafs of wine? He faid, he would juft take what was on
the table, which was toddy: he then put a fmall quantity
of fpirits into a tumbler glafs with water, but was fo uncommonly agitated, that, in carrying it to his head, he
fpilt a great deal of it upon the table, and drank very little
of it. He told me, he wanted to fpeak to me privately;
upon which we went into another room. When there, he
afked

aſked me, How many children I had? This queſtion
had been aſked and anſwered below ſtairs; he repeated
the ſame queſtion again, and walked about the room in
great agitation. I reminded him, that he had ſomething
particular to ſay. Of this he took no notice, but again aſked
me, How many children I had? I reminded him a ſecond
time, that he ſaid he had ſomething to communicate to me.
He then ſaid, he believed he ſhould not be long in this
world, and that, when that event took place, it would not
be the worſe for my family. I ſaid, that was the language
of his preſent depreſſed ſtate of mind; and added, that at
his time of life, and with a conſtitution naturally ſo vigorous, he had no reaſon to apprehend any danger of that kind,
and he might hope to live many years; and I adviſed him
to live regularly and quietly, inſtead of driving about as
he had lately done, which tended to agitate his mind; and
ſaid, that a few weeks ſpent in retirement, would reſtore
him to the comfortable enjoyment of himſelf and friends.
Did any thing elſe paſs? I recommended to him, to think
of ſome uſeful employment, and to take the advice of his
brothers and other friends on that point. In ſpeaking
of his brother Sir Francis, I ſaid he was a worthy man;
and the Major repeated my words, ſaying, *he was a worthy man.*

Lord Juſtice Clerk. You have mentioned a long converſation. From what paſſed betwixt you, did it appear
to you, That the pannel's anſwers were incoherent and
abſurd? He ſeldom made any anſwers, and his behaviour
was ſuch, as to make the impreſſion on my mind, that he
was very abſent. But ſuch anſwers as he did make,
Were they incoherent, or foreign to the purpoſe? I cannot ſay ſo; but I formed the opinion, for the firſt time,
that he was deranged, and not himſelf. Did you think
him capable of judging between right and wrong? I cannot ſay but he was. Did you inform his family of what
had paſſed? I did not make up my mind that night, as it
was a very delicate point; but I went on Monday, and
told Miſs Kinloch what I had obſerved. I begged that
the moſt prudent meaſures might be taken for ſecuring
the

the Major; and said, that the honour and happiness
of the family was deeply concerned in this; for I was
much afraid, he might commit some desperate deed. Mifs
Kinloch told me what directions she had given to Mr
George Somner which relieved my mind, from great
anxiety, which had been imprefsed on my mind by his
behaviour the day before. Mifs Kinloch had, in the
meantime, sent a mefsage, defiring to see me. Did you
go of your own accord to give your opinion, or in confequence of Mifs Kinloch's mefsage? I had previoufly
made up my mind to go, and would have gone, although
the mefsage had not been brought; but I was obliged to
be from home on the Monday forenoon, and on my return
in the afternoon, with the view of going to Gilmerton,
I found the mefsage had been left during my abfence.

Mr Hume. When you mentioned to Sir Francis, in
1790, what you had learned from Mr Lorimer, What
did he fay? He was in great diftrefs; and faid, that he
had got fimilar accounts from different people, and that
he did not know how to act, or what to do. Was the
pannel much affected with his father's death? Very
much. He had paid particular attention to Sir David
during his illnefs, and I never faw a fon behave with
greater propriety, or give ftronger marks of filial affection. Did he remain at Gilmerton after his father's
death? Yes. That event happened on the 19th of February laft, and the pannel remained at Gilmerton, (at
leaft chiefly,) till the end of March. Did you ever hear
him exprefs any diffatisfaction at his father's fettlements?
No. To me he exprefsed great fatisfaction. In particular, I remember he frequently faid, he fhould always
have a grateful fenfe of his father's attention; by which
I underftood, he meant to exprefs his gratitude for the
annuity which his father had left him. On the Sunday,
when he came to your houfe, Did he remain long? A-
bout three quarters of an hour. After you went up
ftairs, did you gather from him what bufinefs he had
come upon? I never got him to tell his purpofe, except
that

that he thought he was ſoon to die, and not even that, until I had reminded him two or three times, that he had ſaid, that he had ſomething to communicate to me. Was his converſation connected? He ſpoke very little, but walked up and down in the room with great agitation, while I attempted to amuſe him, by talking about common occurrences. Did he ever expreſs to you any diſſatisfaction on account of his father's papers being deſtroyed? No. From your knowledge of him, what was your opinion of his diſpoſition? I uſed to be intimate with him: He honoured me with his confidence; and I always found him humane, warm-hearted, and generous; in particular, I had occaſion to find out by accident, that he relieved a woman in great diſtreſs. The poor woman was very ill, and I felt it my duty to provide her with neceſſaries; but I found, upon enquiry, that the Majo had been ſupplying her with money, and that he had done ſo upon many former occaſions.

ALEXANDER FRASER, *Sheriff Clerk of the County of Haddington, examined by* MR BURNET.—

Were you in the uſe of doing buſineſs for Major Gordon Kinloch? Yes, I was his factor for ſome years on the eſtate of Woodhall, prior to the ſale of it near ten years ago; and after the ſale of it, occaſionally did money buſineſs for him down to Sir David's death. After Sir David's death, Did you do buſineſs for him? He gave me a factory to uplift annual rents and annuities, which was dated on the 3d of April laſt.

Do you remember the day on which Sir Francis received the wound? Yes, it was on a Wedneſday. Did you ſee the pannel ſince that time? I ſaw him on the Saturday before, in Haddington, but I never ſaw him ſince that buſineſs.

When you tranſacted buſineſs with the pannel, Did you think he underſtood what he was about? Certainly, otherwiſe I would no have done buſineſs for him.

Here the witneſs was ſhewn and identified a letter from

Sir Francis Kinloch to him, dated the 15th of April laſt, and referred to in the Indictment. It was expreſſed as follows: " See if you can find out the marriage contract " betwixt my father and mother, as alſo Lady Aſhe's " contract, and ſend them *per* bearer, that they may be " laid before Charles Hay, along with my father's will. " If Gordon and Saunders are not pleaſed with his opi- " ion, they muſt judge for themſelves."

The witneſs alſo read a copy of his anſwer to this letter, bearing the ſame date, and of the following tenor:— " Your father and mother's contract of marriage has not " been found, but the infeftment upon it, which, with " Lady Aſhe's contract, and alſo an obligation by Sir " Thomas Aſhe, and diſcharge by them both, making in " all four deeds, are herewith ſent. I have communica- " ted your letter to both your brothers."

Mr Burnet.— Do you recollect of Sir Francis going to Edinburgh, to take the advice of counſel? Yes, I think he went on Tueſday the 10th of March. Do you recollect the reaſon of his journey? Sir Francis told me at Haddington, that his two brothers had found fault with their father's ſettlement, and on account of Sir Francis having burnt ſome papers. I adviſed him to lay his father's ſettlement before counſel, to know upon what grounds he ſtood, as the ſooner he cleared matters with his brothers the better.

Which of the brothers was moſt diſſatisfied? He told me, that Major Gordon Kinloch egged on, or ſtirred up the other.

Whoſe advice did Sir Francis take on this matter? He conſulted Mr Charles Hay. The advice came in a letter. Sir Francis deſired me to communicate the opinion to his brothers. I accordingly gave the letter to Mr M'Millan to be ſhewn to the Major and Mr Alexander Kinloch? but before I had recceived it, I had a converſation with both the brothers upon the ſubject, and particularly with this gentleman at the bar. The reſult of this converſation was communicated to Sir Francis by letter.

Here

Here the witnefs read copies of two letters from himfelf to Sir Francis, the one dated 16th and the other
dated the 17th of March laft. That of the 16th was conceived in thefe terms: " Being only this moment come
" home, I have only time to inform you that from, what,
" paffed with both your brothers laft night it is almoft impoffible that any difpute can arife. I fhall write more fully
" to morrow."

The letter of the 17th of March was expeffred as follows : " Having talked upon the bufinefs to the Major,
" the only thing he ftated as a claim is L. 200, which he
" faid he was paid fhort of the 1500. The particular
" circumftances of one of his commiffions rendered it un-
" neceffary to advance the L. 200, but he faid, that
" though that fum of L. 200 may be fome object to
" him, yet that he never meant to have any ferious
" difpute with you about it ; fo far from that, he is quite
" ready to grant any difcharge that fhall be afked of him.
" He and Mr M·Millan came up this morning with Mifs
" Alfton, and the Major in the frankeft manner repeated
" the fame thing, which I told him I would immediately
" communicate."

" I had a converfation alfo with Mr Alexander on Sun-
" day night, and I am in juftice bound to report, that he
" declared his perfect readinefs to fettle the bufinefs in
" the moft friendly manner, reprobating every idea of a
" contrary nature. In a converfation afterwards with
" Mifs Kinloch, fhe informed me, that fhe clearly pointed
" out to Mr Alexander, that he had coft a great deal
" more than L. 600 to his father, fo that he had no caufe
" to complain."

The witnefs next identified the following letter from
Sir Francis to himfelf, without a date, but marked 18th
March 1795 on the back, and referred to in the Indictment, viz. " I never looked on Gordon and Saunders ha-
" ving ferious intentions of going to law. Their doing
" fo would be more pleafant than talking about burning
" papers, and talking nonfenfe, which can only originate
" in human infirmity."

Mr

Mr Burnet.—Do you recollect having any conversation with the pannel respecting a paper which he said he had signed? I remember, several years ago, he told me that he had signed a paper in the presence of his father, his brother Sir Francis, Mr F. Anderson, and Mr M'Millan, which he believed was to disinherit him.—I told him that it was impossible. About a week after Sir David's death, he spoke to me on the same subject; but as I found arguing the matter seriously would not do with him, I thought it the better way to turn it into ridicule, and said, " Sir, " the persons that you say were present, are all alive but " your father, Why do you not prosecute and expose " them."

Do you commonly keep copies of the letters you write? Yes. Is that the copy of a letter which you wrote to Major Kinloch? Yes.

The witness then read a copy of a letter from himself to the pannel, dated the 21st of April last, and expressed thus: " As you was pleased lately to grant a factory to " me, and to lodge papers of value in my hands, it ap- " pears to me very proper to inform you, That in conse- " quence of the late fatal occurence at Gilmerton, a trial " must take place, and to know from you if you wish to " retain counsel for your defence, which in that case shall " be immediately done, and also to know who are the " advocates and agent you wish to be engaged."

The witness then identified the two following letters from the pannel to him, *viz.*

Haddington Jail, 22d April 1795.
" Sir, I received your letter, last night couched in a " stile not like the usual, owing as I suppose, to the late " most unfortunate occurrence. The reason of my not " seeing you, owing to your official capacity, I by no means " (if allowed to think,) a good one. I do not see any " impropriety in your coming to me once to confer on " business. If after reading this, your opinion should be " still the same, let me know ; and if my message was de- " livered at Gilmerton, which was given to Mr Dodds."
" Sir

" S I R, *April* 22. 1795.
" Pleafe fend me the note of Mr Dalrymple for
" L. 62, 2 s."

The witnefs next read a copy of his anfwer, dated the
23d of April, and of the following tenor: " I received
" both your cards late laft night, and not having been
" informed that you was to go off this morning, I put off
" anfwering them till about breakfaft time, when I was
" informed you was gone. The only thing that now
" requires an anfwer, is your demand to get up Mr Dal-
" rymple's note for L. 62, 2s. The advice I got about
" your property under my charge was, to advance the
" ready money for neceffaries to you, and confulting
" confel for your defence, if you chufe to retain any.—
" I accordingly intimated to Provoft Hiflop, that all ne-
" ceffaries furnifhed to you fhould be paid ; and I need
" not repeat that I wrote you about retaining counfel.—
" I was further advifed, that I was not warranted to de-
" liver up any other part of your property but by le-
" gal authority ; fo that I cannot comply at prefent
" with your requeft about Mr Dalrymple's note. At
" fame time, if the acceptor propofes to pay the con-
" tents of it, it feems to me very proper, to take the
" money, and lodge it in the hands of your bankers as
" part of your property. Your meffage to your brother
" was delivered, but he returned no anfwer. Mr Gol-
" die faid he would call."

Lord Advocate. The Gentlemen of the Jury will obferve, that this letter alludes to the pannel's being removed to Edinburgh.

The witnefs then identified the following letter, which
he had received from the pannel by poft, and is referred
to in the Indictment, viz.

" S I R, *Edinburgh Jail, 24th April* 1795.
" I wrote you from Haddington, requefting you
" would fend the promiffary bill of Mr Dalrymple of
" fixty-

" fixty-two pounds, two fhillings. I do not mean that it
" fhould appear againft him."

Lord Advocate. You have known this gentleman feveral
years. Did you ever imagine he was infane? I have
fometimes obferved him peevifh and difcontentd; but I
never faw any marks of infanity in his appearance, till
Monday the 13th of April laft, when it occurred to
me, from the recollection of fome circumftances in his behaviour on Saturday the 11th, (on which day I had feen
him at Haddington,) that the ftate of mind in which he then
appeared to be, had been in its progrefs on the Saturday.—
What ftate of mind did you think him in on the Monday?
Downright mad; that is, he appeared to be deranged, or
as if the rational powers of his 'mind had left him; and
Sir Francis thought the fame. Did you, fuch being your
opinion, Propofe fecuring the pannel? Yes, I did. What
reafon had you for believing him deranged? His wild appearance and behaviour. I fhould have mentioned, that
I was on my road to Gilmerton on the Monday, when a
fervant met me, and put into my hands a letter from Sir
Francis, which began with thefe words: " I am forry to
" inform you, that Gordon is ftark mad;" and Sir Francis added, that George Somner had been fent for, on
account of the Major having told Mifs Kinloch, that he
had fwallowed poifon, though, whether the cafe was fo
or not, Sir Francis could not fay. Have you that card?
No. What became of it? It was torn in pieces, and
committed to the flames. Sir Francis and a Mr Low,
(who happened to be at Gilmerton at the time,) having
walked out, I was left with no other company than the
Major, whofe behaviour, as he both fpoke and acted in a
moft extravagant manner, rather alarmed me. At one
time, he brought into the parlour a blunderbufs, with
which walked he up and down the parlour, making many
wild motions, and fometimes holding it in the pofition of
prefenting; and I had occafion to fee him put a flint into
it, prime it, and load it with powder. At lengh, to my
great fatisfaction, he carried it out, and placed it in a
chaife

chaife which was waiting for him at the door, and in which he left Gilmerton. But while we were together by ourfelves, as already mentioned, I happened inadvertently to take Sir Francis's letter out of my pocket, and obferving the Major coming towards me, and being affraid he would fee it, I tore it in pieces, and committed it to the flames; and indeed I thought it a lucky circumftance, that he did not fee it.

' Did the pannel appear much agitated upon this occafion? He loaded the blunderbufs with great difficulty. His hands fhook in a moft extraordinary manner.

ALEXANDER FRASER, *crofs examined by* Mr HUME.— Did it appear to you, that all rifk of difagreement betweenSir Francis and the pannel was over, after the converfation you had with him? It appeared to me that all differences was at an end, and it gave me great fatisfaction. What was Sir David's fettlement? The fum he left to each of the younger brothers was L. 1500.—Mr Alexander got only L. 900; but Mifs Kinloch explained to him, that he had coft his father a great deal more then the other L. 600, and he was fatisfied.

Had you any converfation with the pannel about the renunnciation which he fuppofed he had figned? I had; it appeared to me, that this opinion of his was wild and abfurd.

When you were alone with the pannel on the Monday, in the parlour of Gilmerton houfe, Did you conceive yourfelf to be in danger? I felt myfelf in a very difagreeable and dangerous fituation. Did Mifs Kinloch give you any information of his behaviour on the preceding night?

Here the witnefs looked at fome notes which he faid had taken in his calmer moments, after he was informed by fome of the gentlemen in Court, that he was likely to be called upon to give evidence in this trial. He then proceeded as follows, reading from the notes. -

When I arrived at Gilmerton, Mifs Kinloch was in the parlour, and foon called me to the lobby, and informed me, that they had been much difturbed and difconcerted

certed, and even alrmed by the Major's conduct the preceeding night; that he had been very reftlefs, having gone from room to room, throwing himfelf upon the beds. She reflected upon his drinking too much brandy and gin faid preteeding night, and fhe alfo informed me, that he had told her he had fwallowed poifon.

Lord Advocate. I mult object to this mode of proceeding. There can be no objection to a witnefs refrefhing his memory from notes, before he comes into Court; but he is not to prepare a paper, then come to the foot of this table, and read his narrative from beginning to end, and then to go away. That, I fay, cannot be admitted as evidence.

Lord Efkgrove, fignified that he agreed in opinion with the Lord Advocate.

The witnefs was ordered to withdraw.

Mr Hope. My Lord, I truft I know fomething of law, and have fome idea of common fenfe and reafon; and I believe, I know fomething of the law of evidence alfo.

My Lord I admit, that if a witnefs were to take from his pocket a paper, lay it on the table, and fay there is my evidence, and then walk away, fuch a proceeding could never be permitted by your Lordfhips; but the cafe is very different, when a witnefs, after an affair has happened, who becaufe he was not prefent at the accident, could not know or fufpect that he was to be a witnefs, takes down notes as foon as he is informed that he is to be called upon, and looks at them here, to affift his recollection on a fpecific queftion being put to him.

When I undertook the defence of the pannel, I felt it my duty to inveftigate the matter to the bottom, and to difcover every thing that the witnéffes could fay. In the courfe of my enquiries at Haddington, I faw Mr Frafer, who told me feveral very material circumftances. I went to Gilmerton to fee what could be made out from the information of the family, and there it was that I learned from the fervants that Mr Frafer had been there the day before the accident happened. When I came back to him next

next morning he had been recollecting in his bed, and now remembered a number of circumstances that had escaped his memory on the day before. Then said I, " Mr Fra- " fer, put down in writing all that you remember, as " each circumstance occurs to your recollection for as " you did not recollect thefe things laft night, it is pro- " bable that you may not recollect them when you come " before the Court, concerned and agitated as you may " be."

Now, my Lord, was there any thing improper in this?

Court. No.

Mr Hope. Then is not the witnefs bound, by the obligation of the oath which he has taken, to look at his notes ; for that oath requires him, not only to tell what he recollects, but all that he knows or fhall be afked at him. If therefore, a witnefs is confcious that things may have efcaped his memory, he is bound to refort to any means that can render him more accurate.

If a witnefs takes down notes at the time an affair hap- pens, he is always allowed to refort to them to refrefh his memory. The cafe is the fame with a perfon who takes notes the moment he is told, that he is to be called as a witnefs. The notes are the beft evidence he can bring, and he is equally entitled to ufe them.

Had it been, as the Lord Advocate faid, to read a pa- per from beginning to end, and then go away, the matter would have been very different indeed ; but, my Lords, it was but on one queftion that the witnefs had recourfe to his notes, And how does the Lord Advocate know that he is to ufe them any more? I fay, in law, in reafon, and in juftice, he is entitled to ufe them when his recollection fails. I do not defire, that he fhall read his paper from beginning to end, but only that he fhall be at liberty to ufe it occafionally to refrefh his memory. And I fay, with fubmiffion, but at the fame time with fome degree of confidence, that the judgement of the Court cannot be otherwife.

Lord Advocate.—For all that I have heard, I ftill feel it

H   my

my duty to ftate the contrary opinion. My brother mif-
underftood my meaning, if he thought I imputed to him
any thing improper in the activity and zeal he has fhewn
in this caufe, much lefs do I care whether the paper was
read from beginning to end, or partially. I can have but
one defire, in common with the Jury, the due adminiftra-
tion of Juftice. But, my Lord, I repeat again, that my
objection is well founded.

If, in the courfe of examining any witnefs, he fhall find
himfelf at a lofs, and defires to confult notes taken on the
fpot, and at the very time a tranfaction happened, I fay
it is competent for a witnefs fo to refrefh his memory:
But it is not fo with notes taken at a diftance of time:
they muft be taken immediately, becaufe it may be in the
power of a witnefs, by the means of fuch notes, to make
up fo connected a ftory, that I defy the counfel on either
fide to make out the fraud.

I am far from faying, that this witnefs has any fuch
defign. I am far from fuppofing that the gentlemen, who
conduct this trial, could take any unfair advantage; but,
as public profecutor, it is my duty to prevent the efta-
blifhment of any bad precedent. What has been done in
this cafe, may be done in others, by low attornies; not
by counfel,—I cannot fuppofe it of them.

I agree to this, that in general, if a witnefs does not
recollect, he may look at notes taken at the time. But I
demand of the Court, if notes taken at a diftance of time,
ought to be admitted in evidence. I afk you to judge.
I am bound to obey;—and to that judgement I always
fubmit with pleafure.

I fhall only add, that it was held in the trial of Mr
Horne Took, that notes taken at a diftance of time could
not be ufed by a witnefs. The point was long and ably
contended by both fides of the bar, and at laft decided a-
gainft the admiffion.

Lord Efkgrove. There are certain rules which we fhould
never relax. If a man comes to this bar as a witnefs, he is to
fwear to what he now remembers, not to what he formerly

ly remembered. How would it anfwer, were we to fuffer the public profecutor to produce the declaration emitted by a witnefs in his precognition before the Sheriff,
and fay to him, " there is a paper which you have fign-
" ed, read it over, and give it as your evidence."

A man who has been prefent at any interefting occafion, when he expects to be called upon as a witnefs, may
take notes, and produce them in Court; but this is very
different indeed from a narrative taken at the diftance of
weeks.

I can make no deviation from a general rule, and therefore, I am decidedly of opinion, that the witnefs is not
entitled to ufe thefe notes.

Lord Swinton. A witnefs may make ufe of notes taken down at the time an affair happens, but not when taken
down weeks afterwards. There would be no harm in
the witnefs looking them over before he came in here,
but to take them out here, is againft all rules.

Lord Dunfinnan agreed with the above Judges.

Lord Craig thought the witnefs might have recourfe to
his notes, when any particular queftion was put to him.

Lord Juftice Clerk. I do not know, my Lords, that
we would differ much, if we knew what we were debat-
ing about.

That a witnefs is not allowed to take out a paper,
read it over, and then fay, there is my evidence, this I
allow; but it is admitted by your Lordfhips,—it is admitted by the Lord Advocate,—that a witnefs may make
ufe of notes taken at the time the fact happened. Now,
where is the difference, though they are taken *ex poft
facto*, if he is ready to fwear that he took them down with
a good recollection. I therefore think, that if the witnefs does not recollect any circumftance, he has a right to
look at his notes before he anfwers the queftion, and
then, if he fays upon the great oath which he has taken,
that thefe are facts, they ought to be received in evidence,—not indeed giving the notes as his depofition,
but ufing them only for the purpofe of refrefhing his memory.

Mr

Mr Hope. Your Lordſhip muſt know, that thàt was all I aſked.

The Court decided by a majority, that the witneſs was not entitled to look at the notes.

The witneſs was then recalled, and informed, that it was ‚the judgement of the Court, that he muſt not take out his notes ; after which, the examination proceeded.

Mr Hume. Did you mention the opinion you had formed of the pannel to any of the family ? I told Miſs Kinloch that it was my opinion, that matters were now arrived at that criſis, to make it neceſſary to confine him. Before you gave that opinion, had you ſeen the Major ? No, but after ſeeing him, I was confirmed in this opinion, and thought he was actually dangerous to mankind. • I imagined that he would do miſchief to ſome perſon or another ; and I thought it, in particular, very dangerous for Sir Francis, as one who was going near him, eſpecially after ſeeing him prepare deſtructive weapons, having never obſerved any tendency of that kind before.

Had you any converſation with Sir Francis on the Monday ? Sir Francis ſent for me to the garden. I was at that time ſtanding with the pannel in the front of Gilmerton houſe ; and he ſaid, " Why go to the garden ? Let " Sir Francis come to you." I replied, " I will go to Sir Francis wherever he calls me." What was the tenor of the converſation you had with Sir· Francis ? Sir Francis was exceedingly vexed, and ſeemed to be affronted at his brother's ſituation. He ſeemed *affronted*, did you ſay ? Yes, he appeared to me to feel, as it were, a ſort of *family affront*. Was this before the blunderbuſs ſcene ?— It was. What further converſation had you ? A good deal more converſation paſſed between Sir Francis and me. What paſſed after Mr Somner and you were together ? Mr Somner and I, in our converſation, agreed that the Major was deranged ; and I afterwards informed Sir Francis of· the blunderbuſs and other circumſtances, ‑and preſſed upon Sir Francis the neceſſity there was for ſecuring him, as he appeared to me a moſt dangerous perſon,

particularly

particularly about that family. Sir Francis feemed to be, of the fame opinion; and he then informed me, that he had bolted his room-door in the infide on the Sunday night; and I agreed that he was very right in fo doing.

Had you any tranfaƈions formerly, which led you to fufpeƈt that the Major was infane? The Major was owing a debt to a Mr Hepburn, a neighbouring farmer. In May 1789, he left for me with a Mr Veitch, a draft for a fum of money to pay this farmer. When I looked at the draft, it appeared to be for about L. 100 more than was due. But perhaps I had better read the correfpondence that paffed at the time.—Here the witnefs read the following correfpondence between the pannel and himfelf, viz.

Card Mr KINLOCH to Mr FRASER, no date, quoted by Mr Frafer 7th May 1789.
Mr G. Kinloch's compliments to Mr Frafer, and inclofes him a draft for L. 430 on Mansfield, Ramfay and Co. for the difcharge of his bond to Mr Hepburn, and which he has requefted of Mr Veitch to give him on his arrival from Pencaitland.

Card Mr FRASER to Mr KINLOCH, 8th May 1789.
A. F. prefents very refpeƈful compliments to Mr G. Kinloch, acknowledging receipt of his favour, inclofing a draft to Mr Hepburn for L. 430. But Mr G. K. will pleafe recolleƈt, that the principal fum due to Mr Hepburn is only L. 300, bearing intereft from Lammas 1787. And as Mr H. was told, on the 17th March laft, that he fhould be paid at three months from that date, fo the whole fum due to him, upon the 17th June next, will be only L. 328 : 2 : 6. And therefore, the neat way of fettling the bufinefs appears to be, to draw a bill upon Meff. Mansfield and Co. for that fum, payable to Mr Hepburn upon the 17th June.

The

The draft for the L. 430 ſhall be returned to Mr G. K. when A. Fraſer ſhall know with certainty where to addreſs to him.

Card Mr FRASER *to* Mr KINLOCH, 3c*th May* 1ᵗ89.

A. Fraſer's moſt reſpectful compliments to Mr G.K. hopes the letter of the 8th of May has come ſafe to hand, though it lay in the poſt-office at Edinburgh until it was forwarded to Moffat by directions from A. F. Begs leave to inform Mr G. K. that Mr Kinloch wiſhes to pay up the amount of his note of hand, and intereſt due upon it, and offered the money to A. F. provided the amount could be aſcertained; but as neither Mr Kinloch or A. Fraſer could exactly recollect the ſum, and the period ſince the intereſt begun to become due upon it, ſo Mr G. H. will be pleaſed to ſend the note of hand to A. F. and the contents of it, (including principal and intereſt,) may be credited in part of Mr Hepburn's debt; and in that caſe, Mr G. K need only ſend a new bill for the balance that would remain due to Mr Hepburn, after deduction of the ſum of Mr Kinloch's note.

A. F. has taken the liberty to propoſe ſettling the buſineſs in the manner above ſtated, as he believes it to be the moſt eaſy and convenient way of doing it. And he will ſend the bill for L. 430 to Mr G. K. whenever he will receive his inſtructions for that purpoſe.

Card Mr G. KINLOCH *to* Mr FRASER, 2*d June* 1789.

Mr G. Kinloch's compliments to Mr Fraſer, and as the the plan pointed out to him for clearing all accounts, appears to be the moſt proper, he has ſent the note, amounting with intereſt to L. 70, which deducted from L. 328, amounts to L.258, which will clear his debt to Mr Hepburn; and for which purpoſe, he has ſent him an order on Meſſ. Mansfield, payable to Mr Hepburn at 14 days after date; and requeſts of Mr Fraſer to ſend the note given for L. 330 to Moffat.

P. S. In reading over Mr F's. card, there is a miſtake
in

in the fum due to Mr Hepburn, being at moft L.330, inftead of L. 430, as fpecified by him.

Card Mr FRASER *to* Mr KINLOCH, 4*th June* 1789.

A. Frafer's compliments to Mr G. K. acknowledging
receipt of his favour, with Mr Kinloch's note of hand,
and draft for L. 258, amounting in all to L 328, which
will pay up Mr Hepburn's debt.

Returns inclofed the draft for the L. 430, and is forry
that he fhould have called Mr Hepburn's debt L. 430 in
place of L. 330, and of this miftake he had not the fmalleft
recollection.

Mr G. K. will pleafe acknowledge receipt of the
draught for L. 430.

A. F. fent a meffage lately to Adam Mitchell about the
balance of the wood money, but he has returned no anfwer. A. F. thinks, that without diftreffing Mitchell, fome
part of this balance may be recovered, indeed Mitchell
faid fo himfelf.

Mr KINLOCH *to* Mr FRASER, 20*th June* 1789, MOFFAT.

I was favoured with your letter, inclofing my draft to
Mr Hepburn for L. 430. I muft, and do confefs myfelf
to have been much miftaken in faying that you ftated my
debt to Mr Hepburn to have amounted to that fum, but
it was entirely owing to myfelf, in giving a draft for L. 100
more, which efcaped my memory.

Mr Hume. How was the matter fettled at laft? It
was finally fettled in the way I recommended, by a note
for the net fum due being fent to me.

Did the pannel after the matter was fo fettled, ever
recur to the fubject? Yes, at the diftance of feveral years.
In May 1793, when I happened to be at Gilmerton, the
Major took me afide, and told me very abruptly, that he
could not recollect that a draft or bill which he had left
with Mr James Veitch, to be given to me, had ever
been returned; or expreffed himfelf to this purpofe, and
added, that this circumftance had given him very great vex-
ation,

ction, and more than he could tell. To this I anfwered, that I was aftonifhed at what he mentioned; for I was fully convinced, that no fuch inaccuracy or miftake had happened on the part of Mr Veitch, who was then no more ; and as for myfelf, that I was fure that I was perfectly clear, and would be able, on looking over my correfpondence on the bufinefs, to explain it in the moft fatisfactory manner. Did you accordingly give fuch information? Yes, on going home, I examined the correfpondence already recited, and wrote a card to the pannel, recapitulating the import of it. This card was dated on the 20th of May 1793. Did this explanation fatisfy the Major? Yes, I had occafion to be at Gilmerton foon after, when the fubject was introduced; and the Major not only declared his perfect fatisfaction with the explanation, but feemed much afhamed, and hurt at the want of recollection on his part, which had rendered it neceffary ; adding, according to the beft of my recollection, that, at the time the faid money tranfaction took place, he had been much *diftracted in his mind*. Did you not, fome years ago, receive a letter from the Major, dated at London, which induced you to fuppofe his mind at that time very much difturbed? Yes, its contents were fo ftrange as to imprefs me with the idea, that he was in a defperate fituation, both as to his mind and purfe. What became of this letter? It having occurred to me, that the fame fhould be immediately communicated to the family, I fent it to Mr Alexander, requefting, that he might fhow it to the late Sir Francis. Was it returned to you? No. I fometime afterwards afked Mr Alexander, if he had received it, and he acknowledged that he had ; but nothing farther, to the beft of my recollection, paffed on the fubject. Do you recollect having any converfation with Sir Francis refpecting the pannel, foon after Sir David's death, in which Sir Francis exprefled an apprehenfion with refpect to the pannel's fituation? Yes, foon after his father's funeral, Sir Francis faid to me, that he thought Gordon was getting into one of his unlucky fits.

Mr

Mr Hope. I believe the pannel's pocket book is in your custody? Yes.

(The contents of the pocket book were exhibited by the witnefs.)

Mr Hope. Was there found in that pocket book, a copy, holograph of the pannel, of a letter to Mr Francis Anderfon, on the fubject of the fuppofed renunciation already mentioned? Yes, here it is.

Mr Hope. You have feen, gentlemen of the Jury, that twice over, at the diftance of years, the pannel fpoke to the witnefs of this renunciation; and, with this vagary ftill in his head, he actually wrote to Mr Anderfon on the 17th December 1792, a letter, the contents of which you fhall now hear.

Mr Hope then read the copy of the letter, which was of the following tenor: " As I am now winding up matters, and being ignorant of fome things in which delicacy prevents me from afking my father, and in which you can refolve me, I now addrefs you for that purpofe. It is to know the tenor of thefs fheets of paper, which I figned in your prefence here in the year 1788, of the contents of which I was and am ignorant. Though it may appear extraordinary, that I fubfcribed to that, of which I did not know the purport, yet that furprife will ceafe, when faid at the defire of a father, to which refufal I ever was a ftranger, it was done. In my requeft of favour of anfwer, I hope there is nothing unbecoming honour and bufinefs. In this idea I fubfcribe myfelf."

Mr Hope. Have you Mr Anderfon's anfwer to this letter? Yes, it is likewife here. Do you know this to be Mr Anderfon's hand writing? Yes. What is the date of this anfwer? It has none, but refers to that of the pannel's letter.

Here it was mentioned, that in cafe this fhould be thought neceffary, Mr Anderfon had been cited for the purpofe of authenticating his letter, but the Lord Advocate agreed that this was unneceffary; and the letter was then read being expreffed as follows: " I am this day favoured

I

youred with yours of yesterday, and should be happy were it in my power to satisfy you, but I have not the most distant recollection of any papers you signed in my presence, in the year 1788. I observe from our books, that all transactions with regard to your sale to Lord Wemyss of Woodhall, was finally closed at Whit-sunday 1786, and the balance paid you on 27th May 1786. Since which there has been no transaction betwixt us. Will you make my best respects to Sir David, and tell him, he may depend on seeing me early in the next year. And I shall be happy, if, from any circumstance you can bring to my recollection, any thing that may tend to satisfy you as to what you wish to know; but this I am certain of, that I never presented any paper to any person to sign in my life, without explaining the nature of it to them, and making them read it. My best wishes ever attend you all."

HUGH DODDS, *Clerk to Mr Fraser, examined by* Mr BURNET.—
Did you see the pannel in Haddington Jail? Yes. I saw him there on Wednesday the 15th of April, in company with Mr Hay Smith. What conversation then passed? Nothing particular; only the pannel expressed some dissatisfaction with his situation, there being no fire in the room. When did you again see the pannel? I waited on him with a written message from Mr Fraser, in answer to several massages from the pannel. What was the import of this message? It informed the pannel, that, he might give any message to me which he might have occasion to send on business; and he would get an immediate answer. What did the pannel say, on receiving this message? He said, that he supposed he might understand he was never to see Mr Fraser again; and that he could not get a distinct answer, unless he saw Mr Fraser himself.
Did you again see the pannel? Yes, on the Tuesday thereafter. What was the occasion of your seeing him then?

then? To be prefent at the intimation of a petition for
appointing managers to the eftate of Gilmerton. What
paffed? The pannel read over the petition, and (on my
explaining the nature of it,) faid, he had no objection to
it, and figned a confent, which I wrote out. Did any
thing further pafs? Yes; he propofed to keep the petition, and to confider of the matter for forty-eight hours;
but I declined leaving the petition with him, and, at his
defire, fcored out the confent. Did he, notwithftanding,
agree to the application? Yes, before I went away, he
defired another confent to be written out, and figned it.

Lord Juftice Clerk. When you had occafion to fee the
pannel, did he fpeak rationally and coherently? Yes.

Lord Advocate. There are a variety of witneffes whom
I have not brought forward, and I do not intend to bring
forward.

'As for one witnefs, the firft in the lift annexed to the
Indictment, namely, Mr Alexander Kinloch, the Jury
may have expected to fee him here; but after the evidence
which has been adduced, I am not difpofed, and confider
it unneceffary to put that gentleman upon fo very difagreeable a piece of duty.

As to the other witneffes in the lift annexed to the Indictment, if there are any of them whom my brother
wifhes to bring forward in exculpation, it will be competent for him to call upon them. But, on the declaration
which the pannel emitted before the Sheriff being read,
I here clofe the evidence upon the part of the Crown.

The counfel for the pannel having admitted the iden-
tity of the Declaration, the fame was then read. It was
expreffed in the following terms:—

DECLARATION.

" At Edinburgh, the 30th day of May 1795 years.
" The which day, compeared in prefence of James Clerk,
" Efq; Advocate, his Majefty's Sheriff-depute of the Shire
" of Edinburgh, Sir Archibald Gordon-Kinloch of Gil-

mer-

" merton, who being examined by the Sheriff, and being
" informed by the Sheriff of the reafon of his be-
" ing brought before him, and having likewife acquaint-
" ed him, that it was in his option, either to refufe to
" anfwer thofe queftions that might be put to him, or to
" return fuch anfwers as to him might feem beft, he
" anfwered, That there was no queftion could be put to
" him, but what he was ready to anfwer in the face of
" Heaven:— And being interrogated, If he recollects
" what happened at Gilmerton on the 15th of April laft?
" declares, That he has a very indiftinct recollection of
" what then happened, as he was then quite deranged.
" Interrogated, If he recollects having fired a piftol on
" the morning of that day, and at whom? Declares, That
" he has a very confufed recollection of it, but does think
" he fired a piftol; but where, how, or at whom, he does
" not recollect; and that he was in fuch a ftate of de-
" rangement, that he is now convinced, that he would
" have fired the piftol at any perfon that then came in
" his way. Interrogated, as the declarant now appears
" to confider himfelf in a fettled ftate of mind, and
" recollects what has happened, he is defired to
" fay at what period his derangement ceafed? De-
" clares, That he cannot fay when he recovered
" from his deranged ftate, but that he has been
" greatly better fince he has been brought to Edinburgh,
" although ftill at times, when particular thoughts come
" acrofs him, he feels a temporary derangement. Inter-
" rogated, If he is fenfible at what time his derange-
" ment commenced? Declares, That he cannot fay; but
" he felt it coming on for fometime before the unfortu-
" tunate accident happened. Interrogated, If he was
" fatisfied with his father's fettlements? Declares, He
" was fo, and never expreffed any diffatisfation at them,
" but was grateful for them. Interrogated, If he ever
" complained of any papers of his father's having been
" burned after his father's death? Declares, He does not
" recollect of having done fo. All this he declares to be
" truth. Emitted alfo in prefence of Mr William Scot,
" Pro-

" Procurator-fiscal of the county of Edinburgh, Joseph
" Mack writer in Edinburgh, and William Stephens
" Sheriff-officer in Edinburgh; and read over to, and ad-
" hered to by the declarant."

EXCULPATORY PROOF.

Lieut. Colonel SAMUEL TWENTYMAN *examined by* Mr HUME.
—Are you acquainted with the pannel, Sir Archibald
Gordon Kinloch? Yes.

At what time, and on what occafion did your acquaintance commence? In the year 1778, Sir A. was a
Captain in the 65th Regiment, I a Lieutenant in the 18th
at that period; the two regiments were encamped at
Coxheath, and in the fame Brigade. This circumſtance
naturally produced a frequent intercourfe between the
officers of the two regiments, and I then became acquainted with Sir Archibald. In what eſtimation was the pannel then held? I can affirm, that no officer was more univerfally eſteemed and beloved than he was throughout
the whole line, by both officers and men; his generofity,
good temper, fociability, and general good conduct, made
him very popular both in his own and other regiments.

Had you afterwards any opportunity of being ſtill more in-
timately acquainted with the pannel? In the year following,
I was nominated by the late Duke of Ancaſter to a company
in the Regiment his grace was then raifing; and on the much
lamented death of that amiable young nobleman, Sir A.
fucceeded him as Major. This, by placing us both in
the fame regiment, gave me an opportunity of obferving
Sir A. more minutely; and having failed with him in the
fame ſhip part of the way to the Weſt Indies, that opportunity was encreafed: I can only repeat what I have
                                                      faid

faid in regaid to his general character; and in all thofe different fituations, I found him friendly, liberal, fociable and
humane, poffeffing every good and gentlemanly quality.

At what ifland were you landed? We were landed at
St. Lucia, and their ftationed. Was not the pannel feized
with a fever at St Lucia, and what were its effects? On
that ifland Sir Archibald was feized with a moft malignant fever, which deprived him of his fenfes. I have feen
him in his bed in the higheft ftate of delirium, held down in
his cot by a foldier on each fide, and, to ufe a common phrafe,
raving mad. I had feveral opportunites of feeing him
while he remained on that ifland, and while he laboured
under that dreadful malady; and I have frequently been
prefent when he was talking of me, and did not know I
was there.

Do you recollect Whether the pannel was removed to a different ifland, who accompanied him, and any occurrences on
the voyage? It being thought advifeable to have him removed to Barbadoes for change of air, as the only poffible means left of faving his life, Lieutenant Fawcett,
who all along kindly attended him, requefted me to permit him to accompany Sir A. to Barbadoes, which in courfe
I granted. During the paffage, Sir Archibald's fervant
caught the fever, attended with the fame fymptoms, and,
in one of the paroxifms of it, threw himfelf overboard,
and was drowned. I have had feveral converfations with
Lieutenat Fawcett upon this fubject, after our return to
England, and he was of the fame opinion with myfelf, in
regard to the decided derangement of Sir Archibald's intellects, undoubtedly the effects of this fever. Lieutenant
Fawcett is now in India.

On the pannel's return to Europe, did you remark any
change upon him? I was myfelf particularly ftruck with
the manifeft change I perceived in Sir Archibald, on my
firft feeing him in England, after this fever; not fo much
from a change on his outward appearance, but from a
total alteration in his conduct, manners, and converfation.

Did you purchafe the pannel's Majority? Yes, in the
be-

beginning of 1783. What observations did you then make on his behaviour? We dined feveral times together during the negociation. At thefe meetings, I obferved an uncommon change in Sir Archibald, a degree of flightinefs, a wildnefs in his appearance, and a kind of conduct perfectly different from what I had obferved in him, previous to the date of the fever; as, prior to that, Sir Archibald's manners in fociety were affable and conciliating. After my purchafe from him, many opportunities of feeing did not occur; and, convinced of his derangement, I rather avoided than fought them.

Do you recollect any particular opportunities of feeing the pannel after this period, and what did you obferve in his conduct? About four or five years after the fever, I was on a vifit in the neighbourhood of Lincoln. Sir Archibald came to that town. He fent a poft-boy to me with a note, begging I would come over immediately on very particular bufinefs. When I came to him, he had no bufinefs whatever, nor would tell me what he was about, whence he had come, or where he was going. Do you recollect feeing him at Lincoln after this period, and any particulars which then occurred? Yes.

The year following, Sir Archibald came a fecond time to Lincoln, when his conduct was much more extraordinary than on the former occafion. A meffage was fent to me from one of the inferior inns, that a perfon begged to fee me immediately. I returned for anfwer, that not being in the habit of going to people, whofe name or bufinefs I was unacquainted with, the perfon muft be more explicit, before I could determine about calling upon him. Several verbal meffages paffed to the fame effect. At length a note came, urging me to come immediately; that it was bufinefs of a moft particular nature. I was exceffively furprifed at this note, and curiofity led me to go, and fee who poffibly could be the author. My furprife was ftill further encreafed, when, on entering the room, I beheld Sir Archibald. I queftioned him, how he could be fo ridiculous in not fending me his name? He replied,

plied, that he had something very particular to communicate to me; and as he did not wish to be known, he would not
send his name I begged to know what this bufinefs was.
He went to the door, to obferve whether it was faftened;
and then began a long ftory, to me totally unintelligible, fly-
ing from one thing to another in the moft incoherent manner, and talking of projects that he had, none of which he
would explain. Sir Archibald dined at my houfe that day.
Colonel Gardiner, a very gentlemanly and well-bred perfon, was of the party, a perfect ftranger to Sir Archibald. To this gentleman, without any apparent caufe
whatever, Sir Archibald, at firft fight, conceived an
abfolute antipathy, and behaved to him very rude-
ly and in the moft boifterous manner and totally
different from his former conduct; yet, on a fudden,
his difpofition changed fo much, that he jumped from his
chair, threw his arms about Colonel Gardiner's neck, kif-
fed him, and feemed as much pleafed with the Colonel's company, as before he had fhewn averfion to it.—
When he left Lincoln, he would not tell me where he
had come from, or where he was going. The people of
the inn thought him a moft extraordinary being: they
judged from his way of fpeaking to them, and odd manner of conducting himfelf.

When, and where did you laft fee the pannel; and
what did you then remark? The laft time I faw Sir Archibald was near the Adelphi. He formerly ufed to be
very particular in his drefs, that is, remarkably neat and
clean; he then was quite otherwife, his hair uncombed,
his fhoes and ftockings exceffively dirty, (not apparently
dirt collected from that morning's walk,) but as if they had
not been cleaned for fome days. We had fome converfation, but his fpeech was fo confufed and incoherent, that
I could not underftand him. I was exceffively glad, upon
this occafion, to get rid of him; for it was diftreffing to
fee him fo changed, fo different from what he formerly
had been. I may have feen him cafually two or three
times previous to the above meeting, and was confirmed
in my opinion, in regard to his derangement; but, particularly,

ticularly the laſt time, I thought that the malady had en-
creaſed. Do you think that the fever in the·Weſt Indies was the cauſe of this derangement? Certainly. Did
it ever appear to you that the pannel entertained the
ſame notion himſelf? I have obſerved him at times put
his hand to his head, complain much, and ſay, that he
felt pains there, the effects of the fever. He ſpoke of
being troubled with the blue devils, and at thoſe times
appeared very uneaſy in his mind. I once aſked him,
when ſeeing him in that ſituation, Whether he repented
of his having ſold out of the army? He replied, " No, no,
" 'tis not that; 'tis my head ; I never ſhall recover that
" St' Lucia fever."

Had you ever any converſation with other officers in
relation to the pannel's diſorder, and did they entertain
the ſame idea of it with yourſelf?—In converſations I
have had with officers, who have known Sir Archibald
before his going to the Weſt Indies and ſince, particularly
General Tottenham, Colonel Fitch, Lieutenant Fawcet,
and others, they have agreed, that he never reeovered
that fever, and that he was deranged by the effects of it.

In my own mind I never had the ſmalleſt doubt, that
Sir Archibald's intellects were deranged in conſequence
of that fever, and that he had periodical attacks, that
rendered him inſane, and conſequently not maſter of his
own actions; as I am convinced, muſt have been the caſe
at the period of the dreadful cataſtrophe, on account of
which he ſtands charged. I formed this opinion from
having known him previous to that fever, the change it
cauſed in him, and the obſervations I made on his ſubſequent conduct.

MAJOR JOHN MACKAY, examined by Mr RAE.—
Do you know the priſoner at the bar? I do. How long
have you been acquainted with him? My acquaintance
with my unfortunate friend, Major Gordon Kinloch, commenced in Ireland in the year 1767, when he joined the
65th regiment at Corke as an Enſign ; to which regiment
I then had the honour to belong. He was particularly

K   recommended

recommended to my care by the late General Mackay, who at that time was our Colonel. It was there, that the foundation was laid of that ftrict friendship and intimacy, which have ever fince uniformly fubfifted between us. He continued with us until autumn 1779, when he obtained the majority of the 90th regiment, and was foon thereafter ordered to embark for the Weft Indies. Perhaps, this may be the proper time for me to mention the footing upon which Major Gordon lived with the 65th, during the twelve years he ferved in it; and therefore, I take this public opportunity of faying, that he was friendly, generous and benevolent, univerfally beloved and efteemed by every officer and foldier in the regiment, and when he left, it as univerfally regretted.

During the period which you have mentioned, did you ever obferve the pannel liable to fits of bad humour, or jealoufy? No; I do not recollect, that during the whole of that period, I ever faw him ferioufly out of temper.

After that period, did you come to underftand, or had you occafion to remark, that a material change had taken place in the prifoner's difpofition, and that he was at times liable to derangement of mind? I learned afterwards, that the Major had been attacked with a very violent and dangerous fever in the Ifland of St. Lucia, which affected his brain much ; and I have great reafon to believe, that he has never entirely got the better of the effects of that malady ; and I am the more confirmed in this belief, from the following facts, which I beg leave to ftate to the Court.

After the 90th regiment returned to England, at the clofe of the late war, I met feveral of the officers of that corps, who all agreed in opinion, that the Major had been occafionally deranged in his mind, and that his health had never been thoroughly re-eftablifhed fince he had that dangerous fever, to which I have alluded.

In the year 1783, I met him in London, where we were much together; and although I could perceive that he was not fo connected and coherent in his difcourfe as
he

he formerly ufed to be, yet I was not fenfible at that time
that he had any deranged fymptoms about him.

The firft time that I had occafion to make any obfervation upon this afflicting fnbject, was at Mr Charles
Dalrymple's houfe at North Berwick, in 1785. I accompanied the late Sir David Kinloch, Mifs Kinloch, the late
Sir Francis Kinloch, and the Major, to pay Mr and Mrs
Dalrymple a vifit. In the courfe of the evening, Major
Gordon and myfelf fat down to play a rubber of whift at
the fame table; and I obferved that he had been throughout the day in as good health and fpirits as I had ever
feen him in. After we left off cards, we walked out
of the dining room together, when I was much furprifed
indeed to find that he had entertained an idea (as groundlefs
as it was improbable, nay, I may add, impoffible,) of my
having affronted him, by endeavouring to place him in a ridiculous point of view, and to make him the butt of the company; he faid that I was the laft man from whom he expected fuch unfriendly ufage; and that he never would forget it.

The effects, which I had been told, his Weft India fever
fometimes produced in his mind, ftruck me fo very forcibly,
that I was inftantly convinced, he was then in a certain
degree deranged: and although I ufed every friendly argument in my power to remove his fufpicions, which
were as groundlefs as they were unkind and unjuft, yet
thefe had no effect.

Next day, I was obliged to come to Edinburgh, and
in confequence I wrote a letter to Mr Duncan M'Millan,
(who was very intimate at Gilmerton,) defiring him to
fhew it both to Major Gordon, and to the late Sir Francis Kinloch, in which I explained the whole matter; and
Mr M'Millan wrote me that he had done fo. Sometime
afterwards, I met Sir Francis; who, upon the fubject being mentioned to him, faid, that he was perfectly fenfible
that I had not given his brother the fmalleft caufe of offence at North Berwick; that he was convinced his temper and difpofition were totally changed; that he had often obferved him to behave in a moft inconfiftent manner;

and

and that he attributed all this to his West India fever; for he was not the same man since his return to Europe, that he had been before he went out to the West Indies.

In Summer 1790, I happened to be one day in the coffee room at Greenock, and was much furprifed to fee Major Gordon enter. I immediately perceived a wildnefs in his looks, which I had never feen before. He told me, that he had posted all night from Berwick without fleeping, to find me out, in order to communicate to me matters of the utmost confequence to himfelf, as he looked upon me to be his moit confidential friend. I afked him what he meant? upon which he took a letter out of his pocket, and gave it to me, faying, " Read that, " and then be convinced how ill I have been treated by " my whole family." This was a letter from his brother Mr Alexander, acquainting him with the death of their brother Captain David, very expreffive of the diftrefs the family were in upon that melancholy occafion, and full of affection towards the Major himfelf, earneftly entreating him, at the defire of Sir David and the reft of his family, to return to Gilmerton. Upon my obferving, that this letter was very foreign to the fubject he had mentioned, he replied, " That letter is a fufficient " proof of the truth I have told you, and I have no " other proof." At this time, the Major appeared to me to be quite deranged in his mind. I told him, that he feemed to be much indifpofed, and preffed him to go to bed to try to get fome fleep, after his fatiguing journey, and alfo to remain with me at my fifter's houfe, who lived in the neighbourhood of Port-Glafgow; but all this he pofitively refufed to do, and faid, that he was obliged to return immediately to Berwick, where he propofed fleeping that night, and inftantly fet out, notwithftanding I ufed every argument in my power to diffuade him from his purpofe.

The next time the Major appeared to me to be in a deranged ftate of mind, was in Dumbreck's hotel in Edinburgh, four or five days before the death of the late Sir Francis
Kinloch.

Kinloch. One of the waiters having told me he was in the houfe, I immediately went to him, between feven and eight o'clock in the evening: He was then going to dinner, and appeared to me to be totally depreffed in his mind, and quite incoherent in what he faid. I was obliged to afk him the fame queftion two or three times before he would make me any anfwer, and then he ufed to ftart up as if fomething had alarmed him. He told me that he had been extremely ill indeed, ever fince the death of his father, who had made what he (the Major) confidered a handfome provifion for him, and with which he was perfectly fatisfied: At this time he fpoke of his brother Sir Francis with great affection. The Major told me, that he was obliged to fet out early next morning for London upon particular bufinefs. I remonftrated with him againft undertaking fuch a long journey in his prefent ftate of health, and advifed him to fend for, and confult fome medical gentlemen: I likewife told him, that I intended fetting out myfelf in a few days for Buxton, and preffed him much to wait for me, and that we could travel fo far together; but he would not liften to any thing I propofed, and fet out next morning in a poft-chaife, with an intention, as he told me, to dine at Gilmerton on his way to London.

Did you think that the Major's fituation on this occafion proceeded from intoxication? By no means. He called for a bottle of wine, and drank only a few glaffes of it. Indeed his fituation made fuch an impreffion on my mind, and I was fo much convinced of his deranged ftate, that when I went home, I told my fifter, (who was well acquainted with the Major,) that I fhould not be furprifed if he committed fome rafh action againft himfelf.

When did you again fee the Major? I went to the Major the day after he was brought into Edinr. Jail, at his own requeft, and found him as calm, rational, and collected, as I ever remembered him, and perfectly fenfible of the deplorable fituation which he was then in. He faid, he had been much deranged in his judgement for a confiderable time before the fatal accident befel his brother, and that he
did

did not know he had a piftol in his hand, till he heard the report. I called upon him two days afterwards, in company with Dr James Home, and found him, (as I thought,) quite delirious and furious ; and, when we left him, I had fome converfation about him with Dr Home, who was of opinion, that if the Major's fever continued much longer, it would be advifeable to put the ftrait-waiftcoat upon him. When I went in upon this oecafion, the Major was walking rapidly about the room, which was very fmall, as if for a wager.

Lord Advocate. You have told us, that, when you faw the pannel at Dumbreck's hotel, he was alarmed, and that you had to afk the fame queftion two or three times over before he gave an anfwer. Now, when he did return an anfwer, was it a rational and diftinct one? It was generally pretty much fo, but expreffed with a degree of melancholy and wildnefs which I never obferved before.

Captain MILLER *examined by* Mr MONYPENNY.—Are you acquainted with the pannel? Yes. How long have you known him? About twenty-three years. I joined the 65th regiment as an Enfign in the year 1771; and Sir Archibald, then a Lieutenant in the fame regiment, joined us at Halifax, Nova Scotia, a year or two after ; and he afterwards purchafed a company in the regiment. In what eftimation was the pannel held in that regiment? During the whole time I knew him in it, he was univerfally beloved and refpected by all the regiment, both officers and men. When did the pannel leave the regiment? In the year 1779, when he was promoted to the Majority of the 90th regiment, along with which he went to the Weft Indies.

When you next faw the pannel, did you obferve any change upon him? When I faw him after his return to Britain, he informed, me that he had been attacked by a violent fever at St. Lucia, which had greatly impaired his health. Did you fee him foon after he returned? I did not fee him till 1789. We met by chance in the Strand. I was furprifed to find him fo much altered. Formerly he was a moft converfable gentleman, the mildeft and moft humane

humane character; but now I obferved a moft remarkable change. Was the alteration in his manners, or in his
bodily appearance? Both. He was very flovenly in his
drefs, and his hair, which was formerly a fine brown, was
now turned wihte. He often told me, that he had always
been difturbed in his mind fince he had the fever in the
Weft Indies.

Do you think the alteration in his temper might be the
effects of intoxication? No. We dined frequently together in coffee-houfes in London, when we never drank a-
bove a bottle of wine between us, and I never faw him but
fober; though his converfation was often wild, by what
I had been ufed to.

Had you occafion to fee the pannel in 1790? Yes. In
October that year, I received a letter from him, dated
from a hotel in Oxford road, preffing me to come to him
immediately, as he was in a very bad ftate of health, and
had no relation or acquaintance in the world that he
cared for but myfelf. I was then at Huntingdon recruit-
ing, but immediately went to London. On calling at the
hotel whence the letter was dated, I could get no account
of him, except that a ftrange fort of a gentleman had ftaid
there for a few days, and had gone away without faying whither. I however, found him at laft very ill, in bed, at old
Slaughter's coffee-houfe in St. Martin's Lane, kept by
one Reid. I ftaid with him a few days in the fame houfe
till he got better, and then returned to Huntingdon.

When did you next fee the pannel? In November following, he came down to Huntingdon to fee me, and ftaid
two or three days, and then fet off for Scotland. Did you
remark any thing particular in his converfation at this
time? He frequently repeated to me his diftreffed fituation of mind: and he told me fome odd ftories of himfelf,
fuch as that he had gone about England in ftage-coaches
and ftopped for days, where ftrolling players were acting
in a barn, when he engaged himfelf as fiddler to them, and
many other acts of that fort, which clearly proved to me
his derangement of mind. At this time he was dreffed

in

in black (I believe one of his brothers had died recently before) ; and he told me, that he would never alter the dress, as he was determined never to mix with the world again ; and he actually sent many of his coloured clothes to my lodgings, to be disposed of as I might think proper.

Lord Advocate. When you conversed with him, were the answers he returned to your questions rational and coherent? Sometimes he returned correct answers, at other times they were quite incoherent.

Miss KINLOCH.

This lady was in the Outer Parliament House. Mr Hope waited upon her by permission of the Court, to inform her, that she was the next witness he meant to adduce. He remained only a few minutes, and when he returned, addressed the Court in the following terms.

My Lord,

I am now under the necessity of calling upon your Lordships to review your former judgement. I have been with Miss Kinloch, and I found her in a condition which I cannot describe. In such distress, that, by heavens! were it my own life that was depending, I would not ask her evidence. She has declared to me, that unless she is permitted to look at her notes, she cannot promise to answer a single question. Will the Court, under the these circumstances, adhere to the judgement already given?

Lord Advocate. In the conduct of this trial, as in all others which it has been my lot to manage, I have been guided by the principle of public duty. However much I may be affected by the distressed and melancholy situation of the family, I cannot discriminate between the case of this lady, and that of the poorest woman in the kingdom. I must not yield to my feelings: And I will not, on any consideration, deviate from the line of equal and impartial Justice.

That he or she, who, upon a question being put, does not

recollect,

recollect, may look at notes taken at the time, and then make anfwer, is what I fhall not oppofe; but, my Lord, if any thing more is meant, I do fay that it is contrary to the practice of this Court, and would be eftablifhing a moft dangerous precedent. If, therefore, this lady cannot give her evidence in this manner, I muft, however painful the duty may be, object to any depofition which is made by reading from notes of another kind.

Mr Hope. My Lord, fince I began to make the nature of law my ftudy, I have always thought, that if there is one maxim which ought to be held more facred than others, it is, that mere form fhall never ftand in the way of truth and juftice. Now, my Lord, how are thefe to be obtained, if witnefles are to be precluded from giving their evidence, in the only manner in which they poffibly can give it?

We have brought forward many facts with regard to that fpecies of infanity with which the pannel is afflicted. We have traced him in his wanderings about the country, but do your Lordfhips imagine, that thefe were the only occafions on which his diforder appeared? Would his own family proclaim to the world his melancholy fituation? Is it not to be fuppofed, they would rather be careful to conceal it? My Lord, in the cafe of *occult crimes*, the members of a family are always admitted to give evidence, becaufe the truth cannot be obtained in any other way: Now, although the infanity of the prifoner has accidently been obferved by others, yet no one can doubt, that it muft have been much more frequently obferved by his own family. It is therefore an *occult fact*, wich although it has been *partially* proved otherwife, can certainly be completely eftablifhed only by the evidence of members of the family. The counfel at the table, are not the only counfel for the prifoner, your Lordfhips are bound as much as we are to fee that his caufe is not injured;—and is it reafon or juftice to refufe to allow this lady to look at her notes, when fhe has declared, that fhe cannot give her evidence in any other manner.

L

My

My Lord, it is not for Mifs Kinloch, it is for her fex
I afk it. Muft not any woman of delicacy be confufed
and agitated at appearing before this public Court? How
much more fo on fuch a melancholy occafion, for which
this Lady comes. When fhe is in fuch a fituation of
diftrefs,—a fituation, which were fhe not in, I am fure
both your Lordfhips and the Gentlemen of the Jury
would think it a much ftronger objection to her teftimony, than giving her evidence from notes. Will you, or
can you deny her the affiftance neceffary for counteract-
ing the confufion and agitation, which it would be a crime
in her not to feel?

But it is not to your feelings, it is to your juftice I appeal, for what is the objection but a mere matter of form?
Your Lordfhips have faid, that when fhe is on the other
fide of that wall, at the very moment before fhe enter's
this Court, fhe may perufe her notes; but when fhe comes
to the foot of this table, that is, at the very moment,
when fhe ftands moft in need of her notes, fhe is not to look
at them. Shall it be faid in this free country, in this en-
lightened age, that truth fhall be withheld upon fuch
frivolous pretences? Upon fuch a mere fiction, nay
what I had almoft called a quibble of the law? My Lord,
were I the conductor of this profecution, I declare, I
would rather abandon it altogether, than fupport it by
fuch means.

The Court determined, that Mifs Kinloch might look
at her notes, and then give her evidence upon oath.

Lord Juftice Clerk. I was always of opinion, that witneffes had a right to look at their notes for the purpofe
of affifting their recollection; but at the fame time, I think
Mr Hope was rather too warm, when he faid, that your
Lordfhips were putting form in the way of juftice. It
was not on account of form that the Court decided
againft a witnefs reading his notes, but from a defire of
keeping pure the channels of juftice, by fuffering no practice to be eftablifhed, which might tend to corrupt them.

Mifs Kinloch was now brought into Court, attended
by

by two ladies in mourning, and was feated at the foot of the table below the bench. She was examined by *Mr Hume*, who repated her anfwers aloud to the Court and *Jury*; the Lord Advocate of his own accord having offered to take them in this way, upon feeing that the witnefs was agitated, and unable to raife her voice. She deponed, That fhe had frequently heard her father Sir David fay, that the Major had never been found fince he came from the Weft Indies. That one day, about fix or feven years ago, fhe heard Sir David enquire for the Major, and being informed that he was gone for London, without giving any previous notice, he faid, " That poor mad " creature Gordon, is much raifed at prefent; and I am, " afraid that one day he will be in a ftate of confine- " ment." That on feveral occafions, when Gordon was doing ftrange and unaccountable things, Sir David has faid, " Poor Gordon's head is very much turned," and other expreffions to that effect. And in particular, fhe remembers that on one occafion, when the family was at Wooler, and Gordon was haftily taking leave of them, Sir David faid, " Poor Gordon, his malady is coming on." That Sir David once told the witnefs, that Gordon had taken it into his head that he had figned a renunciation of his inheritance, and this he mentioned as a proof that his head was turned. That the witnefs was from her own obfervation convinced, that thefe remarks of her father's were juft, and his opinion too well founded. That in the end of March and begining of April laft, the witnefs obferved his malady plainly coming on, and gradually gaining ground, and becoming more violent than fhe had ever feen it before. That the appearances about him were fo alarming, that fhe apprehended danger to her own life, and was afraid to be alone with, or near him. On the Saturday, Sunday, Monday and Tuefday, preceding the fatal accident, fhe never faw the fymptoms of his malady fo violent; in fo much, that fhe advifed Sir Francis to fend for medical affiftance, and to have him fecured leaft he might do harm to himfelf or others; and fhe thought this

advice

advice fo neceffary, that fhe always kept out of his way, and had for weeks before locked the door of her bed-rcom for fear of his coming in upon her. That nothing occurred afterwards, to make her think that this advice was groundlefs or unneceffary, but on the contrary, every thing confirmed her in her opinion. That on the Monday the Major told the witnefs that he had taken poifon, and took out his watch, and requefted her to take it from him as a keepfake, for he had not many hours to live; and at this time he was in a ftate of extreme agitation. Upon the Tuefday, when fhe went up to her chamber, fhe defired the fervants to hold Gordon's room-door faft, while fhe paffed it, and flipped by, as fhe was afraid he might follow her, and perhaps make away with himfelf before her face. When he faid he had taken poifon, fhe did not at the time believe him, but fhe afterwards found, that he had fwallowed a whole phial of laudanum, which he had taken from a cabinet in her room. That fhe would not, on any account, have retired to her room on the Tuefday night, if fhe had in the leaft fufpected that Sir Francis himfelf meant to feize him, for fhe knew the danger of it; and that Sir Francis had told her, that the Major was more quiet than he had been, and that they would not feize him that night.

Being interrogated by the Lord Advocate, the witnefs deponed, That the family never propofed to take any fteps againft him as an infane perfon prior to the Sunday. On Tuefday Sir Francis told her, that Gordon had been out all night wandering in Beanfton wood, and was raving mad.

Again interrogated by Mr *Hume*, fhe deponed, That on the Tuefday evening, the Major more than once attempted to break into her room, which was locked againft him; and on thefe occafions, he complained that the witnefs refufed to fee him, when Sir Francis faw him, and was fo kind to him.

Mr Hume. Though I have reafon to believe, that a more detailed and particular examination of Mifs Kinloch would bring out many ftrong circumftances in the pannel's
favour,

favour, and though it was at firſt my intention to have proceeded in that manner, yet, in her diſtreſſing ſituation, and as I hope the caſe will not require it, I ſhall forbear to preſs it farther, and content myſelf with the few general queſtions which have been put.

JOHN WALKER, *Tenant in Beanſton, examind by* Mr HUME. Did you ſee the pannel on Tueſday the 14th of April? Yes. You will endeavour to recollect what paſſed? About a ½ after five in the morning, as I went out to yoke, I ſaw a gentleman walking near my houſe, which is about a mile from Gilmerton. He was dreſſed in black, and cried *halt.* This gentleman turned out to be the Major. Was there any body with him? No. What further paſſed? I ſhook hands with him. He ſeemed much fatigued. His clothes were diſordered, and his appearance confuſed, and I invited him into the houſe,—took him up ſtairs to a room, and recommended a bowl of tea and a bed. His ſtockings were very wet, and ſtuck to his feet and legs.— I at firſt conjectured, that he had been up all night at Mr M‘Leod's, but when I hinted this, he ſaid in a ſurly manner, *John, Don't aſk me where I have been.* I rubbed his feet and legs until they came to ſome heat, and then he lay down upon the bed. He ſaid in an angry tone, before I left him, that he would not be wakened.

About five o'clock in the evening, however, being a good deal alarmed, I went up ſtairs to ſee if he was awake, and knocked at the door, which I found was barricaded within, *now* ſays I to the Major, *it is five o'clock ; It is time that you were up.* He roſe, and removed ſome chairs, with which he had barricaded the door, and then he opened the door a little, and looked out with a wild appearance, having two piſtols in his hand. He aſked me, after I went into him, If my wife had any laudanum? I ſaid, perhaps ſhe might have a little ; but he anſwered, that he would take 350 drops, and that nothing leſs would do, for that he wanted an everlaſting ſleep, never to waken. Then he walked up and down the rooin
in

in great agitation, fometimes pointing a piftol to his
left fide, and preffing the muzzle under his ribs towards
the heart, and at other times pointing it to his ear or his
forehead. I attempted to expoftulate with him, but he
faid, (and here the witnefs ufed a loud and pofitive tone,)
" *Don't interfere, John.*" He then fat down, and defired
me to draw a chair near him, after which he beat upon
his breaft, and exclaimed, *Ah! John.* He next prefented
a piftol to himfelf, repeating again, " *Don't interfere*
" *John.*" I afked, if any of the family had offended
him? He made no anfwer to this queftion, but faid,
" *Above all things, I would wifh to fee William Reid and*
" *Sandy Kinloch.*" He alfo faid, he would take fome tea.

I went down ftairs to order my wife to get the tea
ready, and to fend for William Reid, and I then faid to
her, " If a piftol goes off, be not furprifed, for the Major
" is deranged in his judgement, and I am afraid, he will
" make away with himfelf."

I took up the tea.—I poured fome into a faucer, and
held it to his lips, for he was not in a condition to carry
it to his head himfelf. It was hot, and he faid, " John
" you have burnt me." He drank three faucers full of
tea, but did not eat above an inch of bread. All the
while I was helping him to the tea, and holding the faucer to his head, he held a piftol, (which I faw, and heard
him cock,) to my fide, within three inches of my belly,
keeping his thumb upon the cock, and his finger at the
trigger; I was much alarmed, but when I went down
ftairs, I did not let my wife and daughters know the danger I was in.

When did William Reid come, and what paffed? He
came foon after. I informed him of the fituation in
which the Major was, and defired him *to tell Sir Francis
to fend all the men in Gilmerton to feize him, for he would do
mifchief either to himfelf or fomebody elfe.* William Reid
went and knocked at the room door. The Major opened,
and fet it a jar a little, and looked out prefenting a piftol
before him. William retired fome fteps down the ftair at
firft;

irft; but afterwards, on the Major preffing him, and affuring him that he would not do him any harm, he went into the room; but in a fhort while came down ftairs, and went away. The Major came down ftarirs foon after, and faid, " John you muft give me a convoy." I went out with him, but we had not gone far when paffing by the ftack-yard, he faid, " John, there was my bed among the ftacks laft night." I anfwered " while there was a bed in my " houfe, I am fure you had no occafion to lie there." He defired me to walk before him; but hearing him cock a piftol at my back, I was alarmed, and turned about. He faid " Are you afraid John," I replied, " No, I am fure, I " have no reafon to be afraid of Major Gordon." Soon after I heard him let the piftol down to the half-cock, and in a little while I heard him cock it again, and in this manner we walked on together; the Major keeping behind me with the piftol. I now began to look about for an opportunity to efcape, but finding I could not fafely get away, I went on, until we came to a walk, which I knew the Major was fond of. I there took leave of him, under fome pretence, and returned home, very happy to have efcaped as I did.

WILLIAM REID, *gardener at Gilmerton, examined by* Mr HUME.—
How long have you been gardener at Gilmerton? For 23 years. Had you occafion to fee Major Gordon on Monday the 13th of April laft? I faw him about one o'clock in the afternoon. What paffed then? The Major was walking from the houfe towards the garden, when I heard him call to me by name pretty fharply; on which I turned back and went up to him, and took off my hat, which he defired me to put on again. The Major then, with a good deal of agitation, felt firft his waiftcoat pockets, then his breeches pockets, and then his waiftcoat pockets again; and feemingly much difappointed at not finding what he wanted, faid, with a melancholy tone, " I thought I had had fomething;" upon which I (thinking

ing that he intended to give me something,) begged to be excufed, and faid, that the Major had often been kind to me and my family. The Major then took feveral ftrides backwards and forwards, feemingly in great agitation; whereupon I faid, that I was forry to fee him not well; but he made no anfwer, and ftill continued to ftride backwards and forwards, and I left him. Did you fee the Major on the afternoon of Tuefday the 14th of April? Yes. About five or half-paft five, a fervant maid of Mr Walker's came down with a meffage from her mafter, defiring me to come up to Beanfton immediately, for Major Gordon was there in a very deranged ftate. Did you go, and what paffed? I met Mr Walker at the door.— He took me afide, and told me, that the Major had come there between five and fix in the morning, and that he had arms with him. Then Mrs Walker came out, and defired us to go up ftairs immediately. Mr Walker rapped at the door, and told that I was there; on which, the Major juft opened the door a few inches, looking out with a fufpicious countenance, and a piftol in his left hand, and again fhut the door. He had a very raifed, wild look, and his eyes had a very particular appearance. His hair was hanging loofe, and his ftockings off. I faw the piftol, and told Mr Walker, that I would not go into the gentleman in that condition. Did you afterwards go into the room where the Major was, and what paffed there? After I got down a ftep or two of the ftair, the Major again opened a little bit of the door, and faid, " Is that you, William?" I faid it was. He then opened the door, and preffed me to come in. I refufed, unlefs he would lay afide the piftol; on which he faid, " Upon my " my honour, William, I'll do you no harm."—— I again begged him to lay afide the piftol, which he agreed to do; and I heard a found, as if he was taking it from cock to half cock. When I went in, the Major immediately clapped to the door, and put a chair upon the handle of it, fo as to have fome purchafe. I ftill obferved the piftol in his hand, and was very uneafy about it; when

when the Major told me not to be affraid, and repeated that he would do me no harm. I faid, it was his weapons that I feared and not himfelf; and that, if he would lay them afide, I would do any thing for him, or go any where with him. Upon which he afked me If I was fure I did not mean him any harm? And although I affured him that I did not, yet he was not fatisfied, till he had caufed me fwear by the God of Heaven, that I would do him no hurt. He then threw two piftols, with confider-able violence, into the bed. We then fat down; but the Major immediately rofe, and came forward, and laid hold of me with both hands by the breaft, and ftared broadly in my face. He faid, " Where do you think I have been" " all night William?" I anfwered, " I don't know, Sir." He faid, " in Beanfton planting; I had a light from heaven " which appeared upon a bufh, and I heard it crackle." I faid, " like the crackling of thorns, Sir." He anfwered, " Yes, but it was not confumed. The Major then fat down again, and took out a piece of paper, and faid, " Wil-" liam, you have a family. This will be of fome ufe to " them." I at firft refufed it, but, on the Major's infifting, took it, and faid I would keep it till I faw him again; on which the Major faid, " you will never fee me again, " William:" and after fome incoherent converfation, he faid, " the prophecies of heaven muft be fulfilled." I obferv-ed that heaven had never prophecied, or ordered, that a man fhould make away with himfelf. In the courfe of this part of the converfation, the Major took a fmall phial out of his waiftcoat pocket, and faid, " I have taken all " this, and yet am ftill here." I got the bottle into my hand, and obferved, that it ftill contained a drop or two of a deep coloured liquid; but the label was all torn off, except the border which was red. I afked to keep the bot-tle, but this the Major pofitively refufed. What further paffed? He afked me to blood him, but I anfwered, that I had not my lancets; and was very much alarmed in cafe he fhould deteft me. He then turned fick, and went to-wards the bed, and reached once or twice into the cham-

M   ber

ber pot. I was afraid of his going towards the bed where the piftols were, and followed him, and, laying hold of the piftols, put them into my pocket; upon which the Major darted his hands into my pocket, and took back the piftols. faying, he could bear any thing but that. I then afked permiffion to unload the piftols, which he refufed. The Major then fat down on the foot of the bed, when I defired him to remember, that the firft and leading inftinct of nature was felf prefervation; and not to take away what he could not put there, or otherwife, he was taking away the prerogative of the Almighty; he, faid, he knew that. I afterwards fuggefted, that he had better go down to Gilmerton, and not give Mr Walker's people trouble; upon which he ftarted up, and faid, " What, " William, do you think I'm a trouble." I checked myfelf and faid, " I did not mean that Sir, but only that you " would be better off at Gilmerton, where you would get a " good room to yourfelf, and a fervant to attend you." The Major faid, " I believe you're right William," and agreed to go; but in a moment, throwing himfelf back in his chair, faid, " I cannot go." I faid, if he was not well, I would go down and get the coach for him, or at any rate, I would get the coachman, and help him down. But the Major ftill repeated, that he could not go. He then afked me Who were at Gilmerton, and I acquainted him, mentioning, among others, a Mr Low from the Merfe. Upon this I offered to go away; but the Major faid to me, in the moft earneft manner, " You muft not " leave me to-night William." I however pleaded a great deal of bufinefs, which led to fome converfation about what was going on in the garden. About this time, the Major fuddenly afked, if Mr Low was down ftairs, and infifted that I had told him fo, to which I anfwered, I meant Mr Low was down at Gilmerton. With fome difficulty I at length obtained leave to go away, upon promife of returning; and, after getting out of the room, made the beft of my way down ftairs. On coming down, I met Mr Walker, who took me into a private room, and I faid that I was under the neceffity of going home; and Mrs

Walker

Walker coming in, faid, it was very right not to detain me, and that Mr Somner fhould be fent for. I then got out of the houfe; but upon paffing by the window of the room where the Major was, I heard a violent rapping on the window and, looking behind, obferved the Major; on which I ran home as faft as I could, and, after telling my wife a little of what paffed, but not to be uneafy, I went forward to the houfe of Gilmerton. Did you inform any perfon there as to the Major's fituation? Yes. I called out Mr M'Millan to the lobby; but before I had time to fpeak to him, Sir Francis himfelf came out; and I told them what had paffed, and added, that I would on no account fee the Major, as I was afraid I had offended him by not going back when he rapped for me. Did any converfation pafs refpecting the bit of paper which you had received from the Major at Beanfton? On the road from Beanfton I looked at it, and found it to be an Englifh bill or bank note for L.30. I accordingly fhewed it to Sir Francis and Mr M'Millan in the lobby, and gave it to Sir Francis, who returned it to me; and I next day gave it to Mr Hay Smith meffenger, to be delivered to Mr Frafer.

Did you again fee the Major in the courfe of the Tuefday evening? Yes, while I was in the lobby with Sir Francis and Mr M'Millan, I obferved the Major pretty nigh coming under the trees towards the houfe; upon which, after repeating that I would by no means meet with him, I went through the lobby towards the fervants hall, where I found the brewer, and told him, for God's fake, to go to the lobby and make himfelf ufeful, if he was wanted. Did you afterwards fee the Major that evening? Yes, fometime after, Sir Francis came and told me that the Major was in his room, and requefted, as he feemed to have a good opinion of me, that I might go up and endeavour to get the piftols from him, and perfuade him to go to bed. Though I was under confiderable apprehenfion, I confented to go at Sir Francis's requeft; and accordingly went
into

into the room, refolving at once to put myfelf upon the Major's mercy. The Major, however, received me kindly, and fhook me by the hand, faying he was glad to fee me. *Mr Hume.*—Mention all that paffed.

In a little, the Major went to the head of the ftair, and to the door of the room where the young Cunliffes were, under the care of my daughter, who had bolted the door. The Major faid he muft be in to fee the children, of whom I knew him to be very fond, on which I called to my daughter, that fhe need not be afraid, but might open the door, which fhe accordingly did, and the Major went up to the bed, and clapped Mafter Cunliffe on the cheek; but, on my begging him not to wake the child, he came away, and faid he would go to his bed. He accordingly returned to his room, and I went down ftairs, and into the butler's parlour at the foot of the ftone ftair. Did you then leave the houfe? No. Being fufpicious of what might happen, I watched every foot I could hear in the ftair, and foon heard the Major come down; on which I followed him into the lobby, and Sir Francis, who was there with fome of the gentlemen, pointed to me not to let him out. I accordingly ran up, and got the Major under one arm, while Sir Francis took him by the other. The Major, however, got a little way on the gravel before the door, when he juft turned about, and looked up ftaring wildly at the front of the houfe. The Major then returned to the houfe, and, when the gentlemen quitted him, paffed through the lobby, and tried to open the back door; but, on finding it locked, he went up the wooden ftair. I followed him, and faw him try to open feveral doors; but, on finding them locked, Afked what was the meaning of all that? and the butler made fome excufe, that they had been wafhing the rooms. The Major then returned to his room, and fome time after faid, he would go to bed; on which I wifhed him good night, and he faid, " Good night William, and a heaven-" ly morning." Did you immediately go down ftairs? I ftaid in a fmall room at the head of the ftair, and foon

heard

heard the Major leave his room, and ſtepped forward to
meet him, and prevent him from going down; on which
the Major ſeemed difpleafed, and ſaid, " What is the
" meaning, William, of all this intereſt you are taking
" about me to night?" I anſwered, " I thought you had
" been in bed Sir, and am afraid you will catch cold go-
" ing about in that manner." He had many of his cloaths
off. He then told me to go home to my family, and not
mind him; and after this he went back to his room, and
I went down to the butler's parlour. Were you not
ſoon afterwards ſent for by the Major? Yes, on my going up he deſired me to ſhut the door, which I only
puſhed to, without ſnecking it. The Major next deſired
me to lift in a table that was ſtanding at the end of the
room fartheſt from the door, which I was affraid to
do, as he would thus be between me and the door; but,
upon his again deſiring me to lift in the table, I did ſo.—
The Major immediately laid down upon the table a book
which he had in his hand, and which I believed to be the
bible; and he repeated ſome lines of poetry, which I do
not recollect. After ſome converſation, the Major obſerved, that the door was not ſhut; upon which he ſeemed to be angry, ſaying, " How could you deceive me,
" William, by making me believe that the door was ſhut
" when it was not?" I excuſed myſelf by ſaying, I thought
it had been ſhut; upon which the Major repeated the order, and I was obliged to ſhut it. When the Major ſaw
the door was ſhut, he went towards the eaſt window,
and one of the ſhutters being ſhut, he flung it open, and
then put ſeveral queſtions to me. Among others, he
aſked me, How many children I had? and I having anſwered that I had five, the Major replied, " And your wife
" makes ſix." The Major then drew his chair cloſe to
me, and looking me broad in the face, ſaid, " William,
" have you told the people here what paſſed at Beanſton."
I being afraid, anſwered that I had not. The Major
ſaid, " I did not expect ſuch a thing of you, William;"
on which, I again aſſured him, that I had not. Sometime

time after, he wished me good night, and I saw him no
more.

Did you suppose the Major to be the worse of liquor
on the Tuesday evening? No. When I first saw Sir
Francis and Mr M'Millan in the lobby that evening, I
told them, that I neither perceived nor suspected the Major being the worse of liquor.

Dr. JAME HOME, *Physician in Edinburgh, examined by*
Mr MONNYPENNY.

Did Major Gordon appear to be much affected by his father's death? Major Gordon appeared much affected by
his father's death. He had paid him the greatest attention during his last illness. Do you recollect seeing the
Major in Edinburgh, about the beginning of March last;
and what state did he appear to be in? On the last day
of March, or first day of April, I met Dr Farquharson in
the Exchange; amongst other conversation, he asked me
If I had seen my friend Gordon? I asked him what Gordon? He said Major Gordon Kinloch. I told him that I had
not seen him. He then said, he had met with him to-
day; and that, from his appearance and conversation, he
thought him in a very *queer* state, and that he would not
be at all surprised, if the Major destroyed himself. I told
Dr. Farquharson, that his appearance, at times, had long
impressed me with such an idea. Next day, (the first or
second of April,) hearing that Major Gordon lodged at
Robertson's, Black-Bull, head of Leith-Walk, I called upon him about four o'clock. He started when I first came
into the room. I saw that he was in very low spirits.—
I asked him to dine at Hunter's, Writers-Court, along
with his brother Mr Alexander Kinloch. He readily agreed.
When in the street, he appeared to me to be very nervous or irritable; the passing of a carriage along the street,
seemed to agitate him. At dinner, he tried to eat several things, but found that he could not. The waiter endeavoured to solicite his appetite, by presenting him with
every thing that was nice in the house; but it was in
vain

vain, he did not eat an ounce of any thing. In particular, I recollect, the waiter propofed to devil fomething for him, when the Major replied, " All the devils in " hell wont appeafe my ftomach." He could not drink port, and feemed to diflike every kind of drink; at laft, I prevailed upon him to get a little brandy, which he drank, mixed with a large quantity of water. We parted at half-paft feven o'clock, and, in that time, he drank one gill of brandy, or two at the utmoft. His appearance that day ftruck me very much, and I refolved upon taking the firft opportunity of informing Sir Francis of his fituation.

Did you accordingly fpeak to Sir Francis on the fubject? I faw Sir Francis Kinloch in the evening of the next day, after having feen Major Gordon. I told him my opinion of his brother, which was, that I thought him in fuch a ftate of mind, that he would probably attempt to deftroy himfelf, and advifed him to look after him. Sir Francis faid, that of late years his brother had become fo peculiar in his temper, that he did not chufe to meddle with him; that he had frequently obferved fuch melancholy fits; that generally after thefe, he became very reftlefs; and that he would then difappear from Gilmerton for a long time; that nobody knew where he went to; and that he returned perfectly well. About this time, when I was advifing Sir Francis Kinloch to leave the town and go to Gilmerton, as the beft way of getting free of a cold which he then had, he told me, as a reafon for his not going to his own houfe, that his brother the Major was then in a very unfettled ftate, and that he wifhed him to go away from Gilmerton, which he always did when in that reftlefs difpofition, and that then he (Sir Francis Kinloch) would leave the town. Did Sir Francis before this period, ever mention to you his brother s occafional derangement, and affign any caufe for it? Sir Francis has frequently mentioned to me his brother's diforDered ftate of mind as a matter of great concern to himfelf, and to the whole family. He attributed it to a fever which he had

when

when in the Weſt-Indies; as previous to his going to the
Weſt-Indies, he was a very good tempered man. Did
you again ſee the Major in Edinburgh in April laſt; and
in what ſtate did you find him? On the 9th of April, I ſaw
Major Gordon in his brother Mr Alexander Kinloch's
room, at Dumbreck's, about three o'clock, Mr Waite, and
Mr James Home Writer to the ſignet, were in the room
along with him. He appeared to be very melancholy and
ſpoke little. Mr Waite went away ſoon after I came in.
In a little time Major Gordon went away. I took that
opportunity of going with him. I aſked him to take a
walk before dinner. My reaſon for this was, that I wiſh-
ed to have ſome converſation with him upon his health;
but he declined taking a walk, as he ſaid he had a head-
ach, and was buſy preparing for his journey to London,
as he intended to ſet out next day. We parted at the
door of Dumbreck's other hotel. He did not even aſk me
to come in with him to his lodgings. Were you called
to Gilmerton, after the accident which befel Sir Francis?
In what ſituation did you find him? and had you any converſation with him, particularly reſpecting the accident?
On the 16th of April, in conſequence of a letter from Mr
M'Millan at Gilmerton, mentioning, that it was Sir Francis's wiſh that we ſhould come out and ſee him, Dr F. Home
and I went out to Gilmerton, and got there by half paſt
nine o'clock in the morning. We found him in ſuch a ſituation that he could not live many hours. He gradually
ſunk, and died about half-paſt eleven o'clock that evening.
He remained perfectly ſenſible until within an hour of his
death. I ſeldom left him for above ten minutes at a time.
He talked very little, and only once about the accident
which had happened to him. It was about two or three
o'clock, Sir Francis aſked me, " What have they done
" with my poor (or unhappy) brother." I anſwered, " He
" was carried to Haddington Jail laſt night." Sir
Francis replied, " It would have been much better
" to have ſent him to a private madhouſe about Edin-
" burgh." " But you know, (ſaid I,) " that this unhappy
" accident

" accident muſt now become a matter of legal inveſtiga-
" tion, and he is committed to Haddington Jail by orders
" of the Sheriff." Sir Francis then obſerved, " They had
" much better let it drop, for he was mad."——As
Sir Francis had begun the ſubject, I thought it a proper opportunity of aſcertaining a circumſtance about
which I could get no information from any perſon
in the family, namely, whether Sir Francis had laid
hold of Major Gordon before the piſtol was fired." I accordingly aſked him, " Did you actually ſeize upon Gor-
" don, before he fired the piſtol?" " Sir Francis anſwered
" Yes." " Good God, Sir Francis (ſaid I) how could
" you be ſo fooliſh as to attempt to lay hold of a man in
" a ſtate of ſuch furious inſanity, and with arms about
" him?" Sir Francis replied, " There would have been
" no danger, if the ſervants had done their duty." This
converſation made ſuch an impreſſion upon me, that I
inſtantly retired to a corner of the room, took a card out
of my pocket, and wrote it down. Have you preſerved
that card? Yes, I have it in my pocket.

When did you firſt ſee Major Gordon after the accident, and in what ſtate did you find him? I ſaw Major
Gordon on Friday the 17th of April in Haddington Jail, in
company with Mr Goldie and Mr George Somner. My
reaſon for going to ſee him was to afford him every aſſiſtance which I could, as I underſtood that, ſince he had
left Gilmerton, no medical perſon had ſeen him. I found
him confined in a ſtrait jacket ; but walking about the
room. His countenance looked wild and furious : His
eyes were red and inflamed: He was very much agitated;
ſpoke of the horrid accident which had happened, in
terms of the greateſt regret: He complained of much confu-
ſion and noiſe in his head; he was correct enough when his
attention was fixed to any ſubject ; but it was impoſſible to
do this for above a minute at a time, his ideas quickly wandering to other things; and he aſked the ſame queſtions more
than once. I did not ſtay with him above a quarter of an hour.
But his looks and converſation, at this time, appeared to me

N   to

to be thofe of a perfon juft recovering from a fit of mania.

Had you occafion to fee the Major in Edinburgh Jail, and to remark any thing particular in his appearance, or behaviour, while there? After Major Gordon was brought to Edinburgh Jail, I faw him frequently, at leaft once a day. He was at times very melancholy. At other times, his appearance was like that of a maniac; particularly, on Sunday the 26th of April. I went to fee him that forenoon, in company with Major John Mackay; as, from the wild appearance of Major Gordon the preceding day, Major Mackay wifhed to have fome perfon along with him. Immediately when I faw him, I perceived a difference in his appearance from that of the day before.— His countenance was wild, his eyes ftaring, and like thofe of a mad perfon: and his walk was hurried. He, however, behaved very compofedly to us for a few minutes: but, when Major Mackay wifhed him to repeat before me, fome circumftances of a private nature, which he had mentioned the day before, Major Gordon could not recollect that he had told Major Mackay any fuch things as he alledged; and, when Major Mackay repeated the converfation he alluded to, he faid that the Major had no right to enquire into his private affairs, and that the Major betrayed a confidential difcourfe. He became much agitated, he looked very wild; and he put himfelf into fuch violent and threatening poftures, that both Major Mackay and I were very much alarmed.— His appearance and behaviour, feemed to me to be the more fingular, as at that time he was confined to a very low diet. Upon this occafion, I remarked to Major Mackay, that, if the fame ftate continued, it would be neceffary to put Major Gordon in a ftrait-jacket.—On the third of May I went to England; and therefore did not fee him for five weeks.

Had you ever any converfation with the late Sir David Kinloch refpecting Major Gordon, from which you could underftand that Sir David confidered the Major as occafionally deranged? I have had frequent converfations with the late Sir David Kinloch, refpecting Major Gondon, and have

have fometimes heard Sir David mention feveral oddities in the Major's behaviour; and Sir David has often faid to me, " Poor, unhappy man! he is much deranged."

Mr Hope. My Lord, I propofe now to call Dr Farquharfon; and I have the pleafure to add that he will be the laft witnefs. We have, indeed, many more in waiting; but, on confulting with my brethren, I think it unnecefary to give the Jury further trouble, both becaufe it is impofible to add ftrength to the evidence already brought, and, becaufe, judging by myfelf, the Court and Jury muft be very much exhaufted. With 'this gentleman, therefore, we fhall clofe our proof.

Dr WILLIAM FARQUHARSON, *Member of the Royal College of Surgeon's in Edinburgh examined by* Mr RAE.— How long have you been acquainted with the pannel Major Gordon Kinloch? Six years. On what occafion did you become acquainted? I was called to him in September 1789, in Mrs Warden's Grafs-market, where I found him fitting in a fmall bed room, with one of his wrifts wrapped up in a handkerchief, which was very bloody. He was in fuch a ftate of agitation, and mental derangement, that he could hardly give any account of his wound; though he hinted, that he had hurt himfelf by pufhing his hand through the window of a carriage. This appeared impoffible from the nature of the wound; and the gentleman, who had called me to fee him, told me, that the poftilion fufpected the Major had wounded himfelf while in the carriage; and in this opinion we were confirmed, by fearching his pockets after he was put to bed, and finding a fmall knife, the blade of which was bloody; and ftill more, by his evading any enquiry on the fubject, though he never denied it. Do you think, that his derangement was occafioned by the wound? No. I found him fo much agitated,—and his looks were fo furious, that I concluded his diforder proceeded from actual derangement, more efpecially, as the coldnefs of his fkin, and the culm of his pulfe, did not indicate a fufficient degree of fever, to account for the fymptoms.

How long did he remain in Wardens? Several days. I got him removed to a houfe at the head of the Cowgate, occupied by a Mrs Cameron, who kept boarders.— How long did you attend him? About two months. Was he deranged all that time? For the firft month, he was very unfettled, being at times more rational, and at other times quite fulky and deranged, though in a gradual ftate of convalefcence; and it was about two months before I thought it fafe for him to leave town.

Did you ever fee in the pannel any other fymptoms of derangement? Yes. About the firft of April laft, I met the Major coming along the North Bridge very faft, but fometimes ftopping, and looking down. He was paffing me; I ftopped him, and had fome converfation in which he appeared very incoherent. After parting, he turned, and called on me On my coming back he looked feveral minutes over the parapet of the North Bridge, towards the caftle, and, appearing ftill more agitated than before, fuddenly exclaimed, " Good God will that man," (alluding to a gentleman whom he named) " do nothing for himfelf?" On my expreffing ignorance of his meaning, he faid " Will he not go out " of the world like a Gentleman? I have advifed him to " it, as the only thing left for him to do; but I am afraid " he has not fpirit." From this, and the whole of his appearance and converfation, I was afraid that the Major would do fome mifchief to himfelf. This fear I expreffed to Dr James Home; and I afterwards underftood, that he mentioned it to fome of the Major's family.

When did you fee the Major next? In Haddington jail. What ftate was he in? He was in irons, and did not feem to underftand his fituation properly; for, inftead of touching upon the accident, which occafioned his being there, he began immediately to complain of the irons hurting his feet, which were gouty.

Have you feen him fince he came laft to Edinburgh? I have vifited him almoft every day fince he was in Edinburgh jail. How have you found him? I have found him
frequently

frequently much agitated. I never could get him to reft
upon one fubjeᶜt for many minutes at a time, excepting the
melancholy accident; but even from this he would fometimes proceed abruptly to the moft trifling, and totally
unconnecᵗed fubjeᶜt; and, on one occafion, in the courfe of
a converfation about the accident, happening to obferve an
uniform button on my coat, he feized it like a child, and
afked if he could not have a fet like it. On the Saturday
after his being brought to Edinburgh, 1 found him very
fulky, going about the room in great wrath, and complaining of Major Mackay's having ufed him ill, in defiring
him to apply for counfel and an agent to make his defence.
He faid this was a thing which nobody had any thing to
do with, and he would make no defence; and it appeared
very clearly to me, that at this time he did not know
what was meant by a defence. Sometime afterwards, on
being informed that Mr Hope and Mr Bremner had been
employed, he afked upon what authority, was very fulky,
and faid he did not underftand how any perfon fhould be
employed for him without his own confent.
Did you ever hear the pannel regret, that he was not
prevented from committing the unlucky deed? He has
frequently, in my hearing, expreffed his regret and aftonifhment, that he was not prevented.
Were you requefted to ufe your influence with the
pannel, to prevail with him, to give fuch information as
might aid his defence? I was, but could not make him
underftand the neceffity of giving any information, and
accordingly, none was obtained from him.
- Did he ufually make rational anfwers to any queftions
you put to him? I have often found great difficulty in
getting any anfwers at all; and, when I did, they were
generally from the purpofe.

Dr. FARQUHARSON, *crofs examined by the Lord Advocate.*
When you attended the pannel at Warden's, had you occafion to know that he had fwallowed a large quantity of
laudanum? On fearching his pockets, a large phial of
laudanum was found, not quite full; but whether he had
fwallowed

fwallowed the whole of what the phial had contained, I
cannot fay,—though, from the fmell, I believed that he
had taken fome of it,—perhaps a good deal more then
an ordinary dofe. I could, however, obtain no information on the fubject from himfelf; either during the period of
his convalefcence, or fince. Did you ever caution him
againft the ufe of laudanum? No. Did you. find him
tractable? In general I did, though fometimes I was o-
bliged to ufe ftrong expreffions; but he did every thing
he was defired, except to take the quantity of bark and
wine, which I thought neceffary for healing his arm.

Had you any converfation about naming his counfel?
While I was with the pannel in Haddington Jail, Mr
Frafer's clerk came in with a line, which (in confequence
of previous information from Mr Frafer) I underftood
to be a recommendation to appoint counfel and an agent.
On this, I left him and the clerk together; but, in a
fhort time, I was again fent for by the Major, who fhewed me Mr Frafer's letter, and afked my opinion of it.—
I approved of Mr Frafer's fuggeftion; and, on the Major's hefitating as to whom he fhould name, from his not
being particularly acquainted with any counfel, I propofed
to get an almanack and examine the lift of the Faculty. We
accordingly procured an almanack; and, in the courfe of
reading over the lift, the Major named the Dean of Faculty, and Mr George Ferguffon. I afterwards underftood, that he wrote to both thefe gentlemen, though I am
certain, that he recollects nothing about his having applied to Mr Ferguffon, and recollects the application to
the Dean, only in confequence of his having received an
anfwer to it.—He afked me what was the meaning of
an agent. This I endeavoured to explain, but found it
impoffible to make him underftand the neceffity of employ-
ing one.

The Exculpatory Proof being clofed, the *Lord Advocate* rofe, and addreffed the Jury in fupport of the profecution. His Lordfhip commenced his fpeech at about
half-paft four o'clock on Tuefday morning.

LORD ADVOCATE's SPEECH.

Gentlemen of the Jury,

THE duty which you are fummoned to difcharge as a fpecial jury, is of the moft important nature. I fhould be ftating what is not true, and what it would be very improper for me not to mention to you, that an alteration has taken place in the clofe of the evidence, which confiderably changes the appearance it had at its commencement.

The prefent cafe is not one which in its nature is attended with any confiderable degree of difficulty ; or where the rules of determination are not plain and obvious : But I fhould be departing from that which I have always done, and which I fhall always continue to do, in every criminal trial, were I to conceal from you what I really feel, that the evidence in favour of the unhappy perfon at the bar, has ultimately come out ftronger than I was aware of, or expected when I came into this Court.

The Counfel who early in this trial opened the defence with that elegance and propriety for which he is fo remarkably diftinguifhed, was pleafed to ftate that this was *a moft neceffary profecution.* He ftated no more than is true, and what you muft all feel to be fo ; for ill indeed would the criminal juftice of this country be attended to, and much would thofe, whofe bufinefs it is to profecute offences, be wanting in their duty, if the life of a fellow-citizen were to be taken without enquiry, and his blood permitted to flow, without a Jury determining on the guilt or innocence of the perfon accufed of having done fo.

My brother, Mr Hope, in the courfe of a debate which arofe betwixt us, in relation to the admiffibility of certain notes propofed to be given in evidence on the part of Mifs Kinloch, was pleafed to ftate, that, if he ftood on the oppofite fide of the bar, he would not, as I did, have oppofed the reading of the notes; and added, that he would rather have abandoned the profecution. Gentlemen of the Jury, I am of a different opinion. I fhould have violated every rule and principle of juftice, if I had dared to dif-

P

criminate between the cafe of this gentleman, and that of the pooreft criminal who ever ftood at the bar, or have fuffered my feelings for his wretched and unhappy fifter, to lead me from the ftrict line of my duty. Though the pannel has not, through my perfifting in the objection, been deprived of the benefit of his fifter's evidence, whatever force it may have had on your minds, and however much I might have regreted had her diftrefs incapacitated her from giving her teftimony in Court, yet, far from abandoning the profecution on that account, I would without hefitation have called upon you to have given a verdict according to your confciences from the evidence before you ; nor would I, though I might have lamented the circumftance which occafioned her abfence, have confented to an exception in her favour over other witneffes, or have thought that, by refifting the demand made for her of referring to notes, the fmalleft degree of blame could juftly be imputed to me.

Having ftated thefe preliminary obfervations, I come next to the matter of fact. The Counfel for the pannel is pleafed to fay, that the killing is admitted. I could not accept the admiffion : It is proved. And I fhould offer an infult to your underftandings, were I to utter a fingle word on the complete. fufficiency of that part of the evidence.

To the evidence then we come, of what truly is the caufe before you : Is the defence of infanity proved to that extent, and degree, which law and reafon require, in exculpation of the crime of murder ?

The Law of Scotland is, and muft in this refpect be the fame with the Law of England, becaufe both are founded in the plaineft and moft obvious principles of juftice. It is fuch as entitles the perfon who kills his fellow-creature to the full benefit of the defence of infanity, if he can prove it on a fair trial ; but I do fay, under correction of the Court, that it is only he who is abfolutely infane, who is perfectly mad or furious, that is free from trial, and confequently free from punifhment.

He that is fubject to temporary fits of complete and perfect madnefs, cannot in like manner be punifhed for the actions he he commits in the midft of his delirium; but, for thofe committed in his lucid intervals, he is, with exceptions unneceffary for you to attend to. at prefent, as competent to trial and punifhment, as any other man.

But there is a third defcription of perfons, and to this I requeft your particular attention, for it is the defcription under which the prefent cafe falls; I mean that degree of derangement which has been attributed to the pannel; that degree of melancholy and depreffion of fpirits, which, tho' it may border on infanity, is neverthelefs accompanied with a fufficient fhare of judgment to difcern good from evil, and moral right from wrong; which never has, and never can be fuftained as a bar to trial, or a defence againft punifhment for a crime fo atrocious as murder; but fubjects fuch perfons to conviction and punifhment, as much as if no fymptoms of derangement had ever appeared, or as if complete evidence had been laid before yon, that he was in a lucid interval, and in the full poffeffion of his fenfes when the action was committed.

It is unneceffary for me, efpecially at this hour of the morning, to multiply authorities, in fupport of what muft appear on the very ftatement of it, confiftent with law and with reafon. I could refer to feveral; but fhall confine myfelf to two fhort quotations from two eminent authors, one of this, and the other of our fifter kingdom; I mean Sir George M'Kenzie in this country, and Lord Chief Juftice Hale in England; not only becaufe they are known to be writers of the higheft authority in each country, but becaufe they ftate the law and the reafons of it with fo much perfpicuity, that no man can be at a lofs to underftand it; and he has only to enquire how far the evidence is or is not fufficient to eftablifh the legal defence in the particular cafe under confideration. Sir George M'Kenzie obferves, ".Such ' as are furious are not in the conftruction of law capable ' to commit a crime, Stat. 2. Rob. II. for the law compares them to infants, or to dead men, *L. Si quis, F. de acquirend. hered.* to fuch as are abfent, *L. fed fi F. de injuriis,* and makes them to be no more guilty, becaufe of the ' crime they commit, than a ftone from a houfe, or a beaft, is ' to be reputed guilty, and punifhable for the wrong they do.

Quam

' *Quam fi pauperiem pecus dederit, aut tegula ceciderit, L.* 5.
' *F. ad L. Aquil.* And the law commiferates fo far their
' condition, that it expoftulates with fuch as would purfue
' them for a crime, *et non enigas penas ab eo, quem fati infe-*
' *licitas excufat, quiq; furore ipfo fatis punitur, L. infans F.*
' *ad L. Corn. de ficar.* They are excufed by their own
' misfortune, and abundantly punifhed by their own fury;
' but fince the law protects furious perfons from punifh-
' ment, becaufe they want all judgment, *L.* 14. *F. de offi-*
' *cio præfid. it follows naturally, that this privilege fhould*
' *be only extended to fuch as are abfolutely furious.*"

He then proceeds in the fubfequent fection, which I am
about to read, to confider the cafe of perfons who are only
mad to a certain degree ; and ftates, as a queftion of doubt,
the old doctrine argued by fome writers on the civil law,
but long ago juftly exploded, that though they are not free
from punifhment altogether, yet that, by the rule of proportion, their punifhment ought to be mitigated. " 2. It
' may be argued, that fince the law grants a total impunity
' to fuch as are *abfolutely furious*, that therefore it fhould,
' by the rule of proportion, leffen and moderate the punifh-
' ments of fuch, as though they are not abfolutely mad, yet
' are hypochondriack and melancholy to fuch a degree that
' it clouds their reafon, *qui fenfum aliquem habent; fed dimi-*
' *nutum*, which lawyers call *infania*, and the Greek μοφωσις.
' 3. That fuch as fhew any act of refentment or revenge in the
' wrong they do, may be punifhed with fome degree of feve-
' rity, fince they fhew fome degree of judgment. But yet the
' *Parliament of Paris* is juftly condemned by all lawyers, for
' having caufed execute a madman who had killed one that
' had ftruck him two days before ; but, fince he did fhew
' memory and revenge in that act, he might have been pu-
' nifhed juftly to fome moderate degree."

From the ftile of this paffage, and manner of expref-
fion, you, Gentlemen, will readily obferve, that the cafe
which Sir George M'Kenzie here ftates as dubious, not
whether it is exempt from punifhment altogether, but
whether the ordinary or a lefs fevere one is to be inflicted,
is the very cafe of the pannel at the bar ; and fince for that
queftion there is now no room, as the prifoner either is
liable

liable to a capital, or to no punishment at all; you are bound, according to the evidence before you, either to find him not guilty, if you believe that he was, at the moment he took his brother's life, absolutely furious or infane; or, if you think he knew the nature of his crime, to return a verdict of guilty against him.

The only other author I shall refer to, is Chief Juftice Hale. He fays, P. 1. c. 4. § 2. *"Dementia accidentalis, vel adventitia,*' ' which proceeds from feveral caufes, fometimes from the ' diftempers of the humours of the body, as deep melancholy, ' or aduft choler; fometimes from the violence of a difeafe,' ' as a fever or palfy; fometimes from a concuffion or hurt ' of the brain, or its membranes or organs; and as it comes' ' from feveral caufes, fo it is of feveral kinds or degrees; ' which, as to the purpofe in hand, may be thus diftributed: ' 1ft, There is a partial infanity of mind; and 2d, A total ' infanity.

" The former is either in refpect to things, *quoad hoc vel* ' *illud infanire*; fome perfons that have a competent ufe of ' reafon, in refpect of fome fubjects, are yet under a parti- ' cular *dementia* in refpect of fome particular difcourfes, ' fubjects or applications; or elfe it is partial in refpect of ' degrees; and this is the condition of very many, efpecially ' melancholy perfons, who, for the moft part, difcover their ' defect in exceffive fears and griefs, and yet are not wholly ' deftitute of the ufe of reafon; and this partial infanity ' feems not to excufe them in the committing of any offence ' for its matter capital; for, doubtlefs, moft perfons that are ' felons of themfelves, and others, are under a degree of ' partial infanity when they commit thefe offences: it is very ' difficult to define the indivifible line that divides perfect ' and partial infanity; but it muft reft upon circumftances ' duly to be weighed and confidered, both by the Judge and ' Jury, left, on the one fide, there be a kind of inhumanity' ' towards the defects of human nature; or, on the other fide, ' too great an indulgence given to great crimes: the beft ' manner that I can think of, is this; fuch a perfon as, la-' ' bouring under melancholy diftempers, hath yet, ordinarily, ' as great underftanding, as ordinarily a child of fourteen ' years hath, is fuch a perfon as may be guilty of treafon or ' felony."

In

In another passage, this author proceeds to state : " Now,
' touching the trial of this incapacity, and who shall be ad-
' judged in such a degree thereof, to excuse from the
' guilt of capital offences ; this is a matter of great difficul-
' ty, partly from the easiness of counterfeiting this disabili-
' ty, when it is to excuse a nocent, and partly from the va-
' riety of degrees of this infirmity, whereof some are suffi-
' cient, and some are insufficient to excuse persons in capital
' offences.

" Yet the law of England hath afforded the best method
' of trial, that is possible, of this, and all other matters of
' fact, namely, by a jury of twelve men, all concurring in
' the same judgment, by the testimony of witnesses *viva*
' *voce*, in the presence of the Judge and Jury, and by the
' inspection and direction of the Judge."

This then is the material, and indeed the only question
you have to try, whether the person at the bar is of that
description, and whether the evidence adduced is sufficient
to warrant the conclusion, that he was deranged to such a
degree, as to excuse him from the capital punishment due
to a heinous murder. It is my duty to submit to you such
observations, as appear necessary for aiding you in this enquiry : And I must begin by presuming to point out to
you those parts of the evidence which do not bear upon the
defence, and to which, in my opinion, you ought not to
attend : I mean the evidence of the gentlemen near me,
who, much to their honour, seem, at much personal in-
convenience, to have come from a considerable distance,
from the service of their King and Country, to discharge the
best and most benevolent of all duties, that of giving their
testimony in favour of their unfortunate fellow-soldier and
friend. Permit me, however, to tell you, Gentlemen, that
you must dismiss their evidence totally out of the question.
Colonel Twentyman and Captain Miller have both proved,
that, before 1779, the pannel was beloved by all, possessed
many excellent qualities, was polite, humane and generous ;
but that a fever in the West Indies totally changed his dis-
position, and deranged his understanding : The derangement
I admit. But it is the degree of derangement that you are
to consider ; and, unless you are prepared to go this length,
and to say that from the 1779 downwards, to the night of
this melancholy event, he was occasionally, and at the time

of

of its happening, fo completely deranged as to fall under the defcription of perfeƈt and total infanity, you cannot poffibly exculpate him : But the evidence of his family, and thofe moft intimate in it, completely contradiƈts fuch a fuppofition : For, however whimfically and abfurdly he may from time to time have conduƈted himfelf, we have not heard of any thing being done by them, or even propofed to be done regarding him, which can induce you to believe that they really thought him infane. He left his father's houfe from time to time, without previous notice, or mentioning whither he was going : You find him returning again as unexpeƈtedly, and, in a variety of other particulars, aƈting with a great degree of abfurdity, but which neither did in faƈt, nor was confidered by any of his family, as amounting to madnefs. He made two vifits to Colonel Twentyman at Lincoln, where he behaved abfurdly enough, it is true ; but he returned to his own family, and to the management of his own affairs, without any fteps being even propofed to be taken, or being judged neceffary for the purpofe of confining him. The ftory told by Major Mackay, of his having, fome years ago, at Northberwick, taken a fudden and idle whim into his head, that the Major had made him the butt of the company, is juft of the fame defcription, and feems to have paffed juft as much unnoticed by all the family. But it will be recolleƈted, and it feems material, that, on a queftion explicitly put to Mr M'Millan, whether the pannel was able to diftinguifh good from evil, he anfwered in the affirmative ; an opinion confirmed by the faƈt, that though the pannel had been liable to fits of temporary infanity, ftill that was but partial ; as it cannot be fuppofed that his family, when they faw the fit approaching, would not otherwife have taken meafures to fecure him, and prevent him from injuring himfelf or others ; which, with the exception of the circumftance deponed to by Dr Farquharfon, on which I fhall have occafion to remark hereafter, no perfon concerned with him feems ever to have thought neceffary.

Mifs Kinloch and Mr Frafer have alfo told us of other circumftances in the pannel's conduƈt, but all of them of a fimilar nature ; of her father, on a journey to Wooler, having obferved that Gordon's malady was returning ; and that, on another occafion, he had taken into his head a notion

tion that he had signed a renunciation of his right of inheritance to the estate of Gilmerton.

But, upon reviewing all these circumstances, there is one thing which always occurs, and which must strike you forcibly, that you find him living in his father's house, without any steps being taken that make it appear his family looked upon him to be insane. You find him, during his father's life, frequently leaving Gilmerton in a hurry, without telling where he was going; but who is there that will venture to assert this sort of capricious conduct to be in any means a proof of insanity ? It is needless for me to go over this part of the evidence, so I shall not repeat one word of it ; but I shall only say, that, though it may prove a sort of derangement, it does not amount to that degree of it, which, on the authority of Lord Hale, and in sound law and reason, can alone render him unaccountable for his actions.

As to his jumping out of the chaise, and leaving the company on the road to Gilmerton, it is your business to consider how far that is a mark of derangement. You will observe, that he returned a rational answer to the postilion who was sent after him, viz. " He was going to Hadding- ' ton, and he would be found there."

You find him, from the evidence of Dr Farquharson, attempting, some years ago, his own life; but I am much afraid, that you will not look upon an attempt to commit suicide, as a proof of insanity. We have heard of this being done by those who never were either suspected, or accused of insanity; and who, to the last fatal act, were cool, collected, and in the full exercise of their faculties. It is impossible for me, however, not to admit, that the evidence of Dr Farquharson does go directly to establish, at this period, a fit of strong, decided insanity ; and it is for you to consider and determine what weight that circumstance can have on the present trial, and whether that solitary instance is sufficient, in your opinion, to fix upon him the character of madness, in the face of, and when contrasted with all the other evidence, to which I have already alluded, and which still remains to be considered.

We

We had, if I recollect right, one or two other inftances of excentrick behaviour in the pannel as far back as the year 1786. Still, however, they were but inftances of extreme abfurdity ; and ftill, in my humble opinion, does the compleat neglect paid by his family to thefe appearances, preclude any fuppofition of infanity.

There was a ftory that Frafer told you about a bill, which the pannel had remitted him in payment of a debt, on which, after fatisfying the debt, a balance remained due, and had been paid to the pannel ; but which, at the diftance of three or four years, the pannel conceived had not been returned to him ; but, when the matter was explained, he inftantly acknowledged his miftake, and feemed hurt and vexed at the explanation he had demanded. This at the utmoft infers only a defect of memory : But, could it admit of being carried further, the anfwer ftill is the fame, that the degree of derangement was not fuch as to induce his friends even to propofe the putting him in confinement.

But the circumftance which I confider of the moft importance, and of fuch moment, that I muft ftate it to you as of the utmoft confequence, is, that, immediately after he had committed the action, he feems to have had perfect knowledge of what he had done, and was perfectly aware of the confequences of it. The fervants have all concurred in deponing, that, when thrown on the carpet, he faid he would give them L. 100 to let him go ; and foon afterwards exclaimed that he had done an awful thing. When vifited next morning by Mr Goldie, he enters with him into a difcuffion of what happened ; he endeavours to vindicate himfelf upon the plea of felf-defence, by telling Mr Goldie that there was a deliberate plan laid to deftroy him.

From the teftimony of Frafer, it appears, that he was all along capable of tranfacting bufinefs. You have it both from Smith and Dodds, the firft of whom carried him on Wednefday evening to Haddington jail, and a few days thereafter accompanied him to Edinburgh, and the laft of whom faw him frequently in Haddington, and carried meffages to and from Mr Frafer, that he was always collected and rational ; at no time do I find him awakening as it

were

were from a dream, to the recollection of what had paffed during his delirium, and of which he was ignorant while totally deprived of reafon. In the teftimonies of Dr Monro and Mr Bell, you have complete evidence that, during their attendance, they faw no fymptoms of madnefs about him. In fhort, if I can difcover no moment of time at which total infanity commenced, I can fee no period when returning reafon refumes her reign : That he has method in his derangement, and that he does not converfe like a madman, is evident; he has complete recollection as to circumftances that happen fome time before ; and though he may reafon abfurdly, ftill he does reafon, and underftands the confe-quences of what he has done, and the caufe of his confinement.

Gentlemen, the queftion you are to determine comes to this fhort and fimple iffue : If it appears that the pannel was in a fituation of knowing good from evil, you cannot acquit him. If you do not think that he was perfectly and truly ignorant of what he was doing ; if you fhall believe that he knew murder to be a crime, you muft be of opinion that he is anfwerable for his actions, and confequently liable to punifhment.

It remains for me only to offer a few remarks on the only two inftances which appear to me to be proved of any thing refembling that infanity, which can afford a relevant defence againft the crime of murder ; the one deponed to by Dr Farquharfon, the other by Walker and Reid. That they are entitled to weight, and to your ferious confideration, it would be as unjuft as unavailing for me to deny. To your own confideration I chiefly leave them : But calling upon you particularly to confider, and to judge, whether they proceeded from drunkennefs, or any other caufe imputable to the pannel himfelf, or were really the confequences of unavoidable infanity.

That this is an effential and material diftinction, into which you muft accurately enquire, cannot need the aid of argument or authority. Lord Hale tells us, " The ' third fort of *dementia*, is that which is *dementia affectata*, ' namely, *drunkennefs*. This vice doth deprive men
of

' of the ufe of reafon, and puts many men into a perfeçt,
' but temporary phrenzy : And therefore, according to fome
' civilians, fuch a perfon, committing *homicide*, fhall not be
' punifhed fimply for the crime of homicide, but fhall fuffer
' for his drunkennefs, anfwerable to the nature of the
' crime occafioned thereby ; fo that yet the formal caufe of
' his punifhment is rather the drunkennefs, than the crime
' committed in it : But, by the laws of England, fuch a per-
' fon fhall have no privilege by this voluntary contraçted
' madnefs, but fhall have the fame judgment as if he were in
' his right fenfes." '

He then ftates two exceptions ; the firft, " If a perfon, *by*
' *the unskilfulnefs of his phyfician*, or *by the contrivance of his*
' *enemies*, eat or drink fuch a thing as caufeth fuch a tem-
' porary or permanent phrenzy, as *aconitum*, or *nux vomica*,
' this puts him into the fame condition, in reference to crimes,
' as any other phrenzy, and equally excufeth him." And
the fecond is, where an habitual and fixed phrenzy is occafioned by the fault of the infane perfon, in which alfo the
defence of infanity is good. But from both, it is clear, that
a temporary and partial infanity, occafioned by the aél and
deed of the party accufed, is not of that nature as to free
him from trial and punifhment, for offences committed during the fubfiftence of fuch criminal delirium.

It is your bufinefs, Gentlemen of the Jury, to enquire and
decide, whether thefe two inftances are not to be afcribed
to the pannel himfelf, and to the influence of laudanum. It
is clear from Dr Farquharfon's evidence, that the firft of the
two was imputable to a dofe of laudanum voluntarily taken
by the pannel : And the evidence of Mifs Kinloch, joined
to the teftimony of Reid, who faw him on the Tuefday
evening, with a phial, in which a fmall quantity of high
coloured liquid remained, afford convincing evidence that his
deranged ftate muft have in a great meafure, perhaps wholly,
been owing to the fame caufe. Had he, on this laft occafion,
for the firft time experienced the effeçts of that dofe, even
then, would the authority of Lord Hale have applied to his
cafe, and difabled him from pleading the delirium as an excufe. But, having once, on a former occafion, fuffered fo
feverely, he muft have known, and is to be prefumed to
have

have known, when he fwallowed the fecond, that fimilar
confequences muft inevitably follow; and it is for you to
confider, whether that circumftance does not oblige you to
hold him ftill more directly accountable.

To myfelf, Gentlemen, it appears to be proved, that the
pannel was, from the Weft India fever downward, often in a
ftate of derangement, but that attended with a fufficient degree of reafon; and that from the year 1779, till he appears early on the Tuefday morning at the houfe of Beanfton, or, at furtheft, till he appears on the preceding Sunday
at Mr Goldie's manfe, there is not the fmalleft veftige of
proof, to fatisfy you that he was in that ftate of lunacy,
which alone can entitle you to fuftain the defence. The
evidence of Mifs Kinloch, of Walker, and of Reid, as to his
conduct and demeanour for the two days previous to the
fatal act, is of a nature different from what appears at an
earlier period; and upon its weight and fufficiency you
will, giving due attention to the obfervations I have made,
determine with impartiality, and according to the dictates
of your own confcience.

Gentlemen of the Jury, I have thus gone over a cafe
which I ftated in the outfet as attended with fome degree
of difficulty, and on what that difficulty is founded I have
endeavoured to explain. It is but fair I fhould acknowledge, that there are many circumftances attending his conduct during the 48 hours prior to the event, which are favourable to the defence; and the evidence of Dr Home, of
what paffed betwixt him and the late Sir Francis, is of the
fame nature. It is for you, Gentlemen, to confider what
weight thefe circumftances ought to have, when contrafted
with thofe which I have already fuggefted for your confideration. If he had been really infane, it certainly was the
duty of his friends to have taken long ago the neceffary
and proper fteps for having him fecured; even ftill, they
have not advifed him to plead that in defence. He admits
that he is fane and well at this moment, and that he is competent to ftand trial before you. The rapidity of his recovery from the alledged ftate of infanity, and the very fhort
duration of it, if it exifted at all, or to a fufficient degree
to exculpate, are now the fubject of your impartial and ferious deliberation.

To

To thofe falfe, idle, and indecent reports, which I under=
ftand have been circulated out of doors, refpecting this
trial, you, Gentlemen, will pay as little attention as I do.
You know your duty too well, and what juftice requires of
you, to be biaffed on either fide in a queftion of this nature, or to be influenced by any thing but the evidence laid
before you. We were told, to the aftonifhment of us all,
in the commencement of this trial, that even the pulpit itfelf had been made the channel of mifreprefentation. Be
the man who he may, ye cannot but join in feeling indignation at his folly and indecency, who dared on the eve of a
folemn trial to anticipate the verdict of an impartial jury,
or touch upon a fubject which I thought every man had
felt to be facred from difcuffion. Gentlemen, if any of
you have heard thefe reports, or liftened to fuch a preach-
er, I am fenfible you will difregard them ; you will look
only to the evidence before you, and decide upon it like
honeft men.

That the evidence has come out more favourably for
the defence, than I had reafon to expect, a feeling of juftice has already compelled me to acknowledge. Where
the force of thefe is weakened, and what are the topics, to
which you, on the part of the public, ought to attend, I
have endeavoured to point out : Should the refult be, to
balance the whole nearly equally on your minds, God for-
bid, that, where the life of a fellow-creature is concerned, I
fhould attempt to perfuade you, were the attempt likely
to fucceed, that the fcale fhould not be inclined to the fide
of mercy.

Mr HOPE's SPEECH.

My Lord Juſtice Clerk, and Gentlemen of the Jury,

I FEEL myſelf greatly agitated. I have waited with extreme impatience for the preſent moment ; and, now that it is come, I wiſh I may have either ſtrength or recollection to give utterance to the multitude of ideas which crowd upon me : the ſubject really overcomes me, and I hard know how or where to begin.

You have heard a very ingenious ſpeech from the learned Lord, and I muſt in juſtice add, a very candid one ; a ſpeech, in point of candour, juſt what I expected, and every way becoming his honourable mind : Indeed, his candour ſeemed to be at variance with his duty and abilities, and evidently betrayed him into inconſiſtencies, which even his eloquence could not diſguiſe. But, before proceeding to reply to him, or to give you my own obſervations on this caſe, there is one preliminary view of it which I cannot refrain from giving you, becauſe it has made the ſtrongeſt impreſſion on myſelf : It is indeed affecting beyond meaſure, and teaches how vain and fleeting are even thoſe enjoyments here, which we are the beſt entitled to call our own.

Gentlemen, I deſire to call to your remembrance the honourable teſtimony which you have heard of the priſoner's character prior to 1780, and to contraſt it with the ſubſequent melancholy change. See him entering early into the army, the ſecond ſon of an honourable houſe, himſelf poſſeſſed of an independent fortune, embracing the profeſſion of a ſoldier, for glory, not for profit, and devoting himſelf to the ſervice of his country, only for his country's ſake : See him entering into that profeſſion, of all reſpectable profeſſions the moſt reſpectable, himſelf the moſt reſpected officer in the line. You heard the character which was given of him by thoſe who knew him well, who have come from the extremities of the Iſland, to which the ſummons of this Court could not have reached them, voluntarily, to ſupport a fellow ſoldier in diſtreſs, and who, by doing juſtice to his character for friendſhip, generoſity, benevolence, humanity, and every ſocial and amiable accompliſhment, have, in the moſt decided

ed

ed manner, proved their own title to fhare in the praifes they beftowed. " Beloved and efteemed in his own regi-
' ment by both officers and men, refpected by the whole
' line, and in every point one of the moft amiable characters
' they ever knew,"' were the words of his companions :
Noble and generous friends ! I know not whether to admire
moft, yourfelves who give, or your now unhappy friend
who deferves fuch teftimony.

Such was Major Gordon, when in 1780 he failed
to the Weft Indies, to that malignant and accurfed
climate, which has been the grave of millions, and which
feems to have been ceded to Europeans by the wrath of
Heaven, to be a fcourge and punifhment for the horrid
barbarities they have acted there. Such was he, when
he failed, commanding a regiment of his brave country-
men, all flourifhing like himfelf in youth, and health,
and fpirits. ' View now the difmal melancholy change : By
heavens ! I cannot bear it ; O God, thy ways are juft, but
fure they are infcrutable ! If virtue, honour, and humanity,
ever deferved thy favour, or entitled their poffeffors to fuccefs and profperity in this life, as well as happinefs hereafter, furely the prifoner would have been the object of thy
care : But let me not blafpheme, thy purpofes muft be ferved, thy will be done.

Turn then, Gentlemen, to the fad reverfe. View the
prifoner now ftretched on the bed of ficknefs and of
phrenzy ; nurfed and attended by thofe friends who
have here borne teftimony in his favour, and whofe
friendfhip, the danger of contagion could not deter from
adminiftering to his relief. View him, by their care, re-
ftored again to life, only to curfe the care which had
fnatched him from the grave. View him now returned to
Britain, alas ! how changed ; changed, not in reafon only, but
in his very nature ; the whole man abfolutely loft ; and the
amiable and generous Gordon Kinloch, become the fullen,
morofe, jealous, and troublefome being, which he has fince
occafionally exifted. See him often a plague and affront to
that family of which he was once the flower ; fee him fhunned
and avoided as a peft, by thofe very perfons who once court-
ed his company, and thought themfelves honoured by his
friendfhip ; fee him wandering from his father's houfe,
coming he knows not whence, going he knows not where,
but

but in all places an object of terror and averfion. View at
laft the concluding fcene of this fad tragedy,—his brother
fallen by his hand,—himfelf now anfwering for his murder;
think on this fad change, and let it make you ferious; think
on the prifoner's fate, then think of the bleffings which
yourfelves enjoy, and let it make you grateful.

But, Gentlemen, miftake me not; think not that I have
thus appealed to your feelings, becaufe I have need of your
compaffion. I defire not mercy, unlefs you can give it me
with juftice; I do not think I have occafion to throw the
picture I have drawn into the fcale; though furely, if the
fcales were even, it would indeed turn the balance. I have
dwelt on this fubject, not fo much for the prifoner's fake,
as for our own. It has taught me a leffon of humility,
which I fhall not eafily forget, and which none of you perhaps may be the worfe to learn. It may teach us all to
acknowledge, what all already know, that even our characters are not our own, and that our very virtues, as well
as the faculties and powers of the body and mind, are fubject to difeafe, to alteration and decay. It may teach us, too,
how uncertain and worthlefs a reward is often human
praife. At the other end of the ifland, Parliament is now
employed in erecting a monument to one great man, who,
perhaps fortunately for himfelf, died in that infernal climate; while you are defired to doom to death and infamy
one not lefs amiable, who unhappily furvived it.

But I will not longer diftrefs your feelings, to which I
have no occafion to appeal; neither will I wafte your time
in guarding you againft thofe prejudices, which I know you
muft have imbibed in confequence of the innumerable and
infamous calumnies which were propagated on this fubject.
If you had brought the moft inveterate prejudices into Court,
I am fure they muft foon have been effaced; for certain I am,
that the firft two hours of this trial, if not fufficient to clear
the prifoner, were enough to convince you how vilely he
has been abufed; by none more than by myfelf; not, indeed, by propagating the calumnies which I heard, but by
too eafily believing them: Believing to fuch a degree, that
I at firft refufed to be his Counfel; and at laft only confented at the requeft of a common and refpected relation. But
the very firft enquiry which I made into this affair, fatisfied

fied me, how much injuſtice I had done the priſoner, and I
truſtthis day that I ſhall make him reparation.

Gentlemen, fatigued as we are, I ſhall not trouble you
with going into the evidence in detail. I ſhall take the
great features of this cauſe, referring to the particulars of
the evidence, only in ſo far as may be neceſſary to confirm
the arguments which I ſhall advance.

But, before proceeding to the evidence, it is neceſſary to
ſay a word, and but a word, on the law as laid down to you
by the learned Lord: I ſhall not pretend to enter the liſts
of definition either with the learned Lord himſelf, with
M'Kenzie, or with Hale; they are all great and able men;
but I ſuſpect much that they are better lawyers than phyſi-
cians, and that they have given way too much to a profeſſional propenſity to ſubdivide and methodiſe. For my part,
I ſhall not attempt to reduce madneſs to fixed rules; nor to
define the different kinds and degrees of it, which I have
always found to be as numerous and diverſified as the unhappy perſons who were the ſubjects of the diſorder. I
ſhall not ſpeak to you in technical language, which none of
us probably underſtand, and which, unapplied to particular
caſes, and unexplained by examples, conveys to my mind no
poſitive and preciſe ideas. Indeed, after all the learned diviſions and ſub-diviſions of M'Kenzie and Hale, they are both
obliged to confeſs, that, theſe notwithſtanding, the Jury muſt
judge from the circumſtances of each particular caſe. For
my part, I think there is but one juſt and practical obſervation on this ſubject in either of their works: That, whatever may be the general and ordinary degree or ſymptoms
of the diſorder in the patient, if a total inſanity be upon
him at the time, it excludes the poſſibility of guilt or of
puniſhment. This is common ſenſe, and it can be reduced
into practice. By this rule I deſire you to try the priſoner;
and, if you wiſh for a definition either of the kind or degree
of his inſanity, you will find a better one in the evidence
before you, than in the abſtract and ſpeculative definitions
of M'Kenzie or Hale. If you wiſh for the *kind* or ſpecies
of his madneſs, the witneſſes will tell you, it was of that
kind as to make them apprehend miſchief either to himſelf
or to others; to make *him* apprehend plots, and miſchief,

R   and

and danger from all around him, particularly his beſt friends, which Dr Monro told you was the never-failing and ſtrongeſt ſymptom of entire madneſs. It was of that kind that made Somner ſay, he had no doubt that he would have ſhot any perſon who attempted to ſeize him ; it was of that kind, which made Fraſer think him " *dangerous to mankind.*" Deſcriptions like theſe, from perſons who witneſſed his behaviour, are worth all the diviſions and definitions of the learned Lord, and his two learned authors.

If you wiſh for the *degree* of his diſorder, it is in ſome meaſure implied in the above deſcription of its kind, and can be further read in the advice which every perſon gave to confine him, and in the preparations which the family had actually made for coercion. Indeed, his madneſs ſeems to have paſſed *degrees*, and to have arrived at its *criſis*, as Fraſer emphatically termed it.

If therefore, Gentlemen, you are ſatisfied, from a review of the evidence, that his caſe does correſpond with the above deſcription of it, you will acquit the priſoner, although you ſhould not- find his caſe to agree exactly with the preſumptuous definitions of the lawyers : Preſumption indeed ! to attempt to trace the infinite varieties of a diſordered imagination, which, even in its ſound and natural ſtate, is the moſt boundleſs and unfettered faculty of the human mind. We, Gentlemen, will purſue a humbler and a ſafer path; and, inſtead of endeavouring to arrange, and claſs, and define and limit madneſs, we will endeavour to trace its progreſs and effects in one individual unhappily afflicted with it.

I ſhall now, Gentlemen, proceed more directly to the caſe; and I wiſh firſt to call your particular attention to an argument and admiſſion of the learned Lord, while it is freſh in your recollection, and of which I wiſh you never to loſe ſight. It is deciſive of the caſe for the priſoner ; and I was aſtoniſhed that the learned Lord could dwell on the topic ſo long, without obſerving the fallacy of his argument.

He admitted that it was proved by a variety of witneſſes, particularly the gentlemen from England, that the priſoner prifoner had been frequently deranged to a very confider-able degree. But he contended, that their teftimony muft be thrown entirely afide ; becaufe, whatever was the actual degree of derangement to which the pannel had formerly been liable, his relations, who are proved to have known of it, did not conceive it to be total or dangerous, becaufe it was proved that they had never thought of taking any mea-fures for fecuring him. Now, this certainly proves, as the learned Lord has juftly ftated, that his derangement had never before, (except in the inftance fworn to by Dr Far-quharfon), amounted to total and abfolute infanity—That his difeafe had never before come to a *crifis*, to ufe the em-phatical words of Mr Frafer—That his relations were not afraid of mifchief from him, at leaft to others. But, becaufe he never *before was* totally and dangeroufly infane, could any perfon have juftly concluded that he never *would* be fo ; or is it any proof that he was not *at the time* of this ac-cident ? I admit, in the words of the learned Lord, to which I beg to refer you while they are frefh in your recollection, that his derangement on former occafions does not appear to have made fuch an *impreffion* on the family, as to fug-geft to them the propriety or neceffity of adopting any mode of coercion. I admit with the learned Lord, that the im-preffion which his family had of his former attacks, is the beft evidence we can have of their nature and degree. In this admiffion, I perfectly agree with my learned friend. I defire to prefs it moft earneftly upon you, for it is an ad-miffion from which I will not fuffer him to depart. But, if the impreffion which his difeafe made on his family on former occafions, is to be evidence that he was not totally mad, what will the learned Lord make of the impreffion and conduct of the family on the laft occafion ? What will he make of the very fame impreffion entertained by every friend of the family ? What will he make of the advice which they received from thofe friends, whether of the pro-feffion or not ? If the impreffion which his fituation made on the family is to be evidence, and it certainly is the beft, then what was their impreffiqn at the time of the melancholy event ? Is it not proved that every member of the family was convinced of the abfolute neceffity of immediately fecuring him ? Is it not proved that every friend who faw him was of the fame opinion ? Is it not

proved

proved that they gave the family, and in particular Sir
Francis, information of their opinion, accompanied with the
moſt earneſt and decided advice? Was not this advice ſecond-
ed by their medical friends, who, to' the common obſervation of mankind, added the certainty of ſcience and experience? Did not this impreſſion travel with the priſoner
from place to place? Wherever he was ſeen, did not perſons,
without communication or concert, inſtantly conceive the
ſame opinion of him? He is ſeen in Edinburgh as early as
the 28th March by Dr Home and Dr Farquharſon, who
communicate their obſervations of his malady to each other.
Dr Home informs Sir Francis, who inſtantly tells him he
had obſerved the ſame. The priſoner goes to Gilmerton;
his ſituation is remarked by his ſiſter, who communicates
it to Mr Somner; but ſhe only tells Somner what he had
obſerved before. He goes to Mr Goldie's, who forms a
decided opinion that he ought to be ſecured; Mr Goldie
goes to Gilmerton to impart this opinion to Miſs Kinloch,
who meets him only by telling him that ſhe had already
anticipated his advice, and had ſent for Somner. Somner
and Fraſer come to Gilmerton on the Monday morning,
and not only adviſe, but urge and expoſtulate with them
on the neceſſity of ſecuring him. At laſt, on the fatal night,
Walker ſends from Beanſton a meſſage by Reid, to ſend up
all the ſervants for that purpoſe; and Reid, in the very act
of delivering the meſſage, is frightened by the priſoner's appearance. In the courſe of the evening, M'Millan interpoſes
with ſimilar advice, and obtains permiſſion to write for
Somner; and how does he write? he writes as of a matter
perfectly familiar, and of which they were all perfectly
aware. He deſires him to come immediately, and bring
with him *what is neceſſary*. Does this appear vague and
inexplicit to Somner? Is he at any loſs to interpret it?
No; and how does he interpret it? he underſtands it at
once to mean a keeper and a ſtrait waiſtcoat; ſo well did he
know what the family thought, and what they had intended
to do. When he comes with the apparatus, does he retract
his advice, or do the family alter their opinion? Is their
" impreſſion," to uſe the learned Lord's favourite word,
altered or diminiſhed? No; Somner continues to adviſe, and
they to reſolve: not ſatisfied with the aſſiſtance in the
houſe of three or four men ſervants, beſides a poſt-boy from
Haddington,

Haddington, they fend for three labourers from the farm. Here is another impreffion for the learned Lord, an impreffion of danger, as well as of neceffity. They muft have feen ten thoufand circumftances in his behaviour, which cannot be conveyed to you by defcription, before it would have been thought neceffary to take fuch precautions as thefe. But we are told that the farm fervants were difmiffed, and this is given as a proof that coercion was abandoned. If it was, the event only proves that it was moft *foolifhly* abandoned; but the contrary is proved; it is indeed true, that the labourers were difmiffed, under the delufion of a momentary calm ; but is it not proved, that in a few minutes they were again convinced of the neceffity of coercion ? Is it not proved, that, after his firft appearance in the parlour, the fervants were called in, and defired to be in readinefs in cafe of his return. When he did return, and Sir Francis followed to fecure him, I have no doubt that he expected to find the fervants ftanding ready to affift ; indeed this is clear from what, in his dying moments, he faid to Dr Home; not finding them there, he attempted it by himfelf, and by his other brother Alexander ; and well might he acknowledge, it was madnefs to do fo.

Such, then, was the impreffion of the family on this occafion of the abfolute neceffity of fecuring him. Had it been an " *impreffion*" only, I fhould have maintained it to be good evidence, even although, from falfe delicacy or other motives, it had never gone beyond an impreffion. But, in fact, you fee them fo perfectly fatisfied that their impreffion was right, that they proceeded to act upon it, by making moft wife and falutary preparations, and then fpoiling all by an injudicious and ineffectual attempt.

But their *attempt*, though fatal to themfelves, is fufficient for me. It is better than even the learned Lord's " impreffion;" and proves to demonftration, that they were fully fatisfied of the truth of the opinion they had formed, both on the degree of his derangement, and the neceffity of coercion.

And now, Gentlemen, in the face of all this evidence, in oppofition to the opinion of every friend who faw him ; in
oppofition

opposition to the advice of every professional person consulted on the occasion; in opposition to the impression of the family, to the attempt of Sir Francis; you, sitting here, wanting the strong evidence which they had, his eyes, his looks, his gestures, his tones, his whole demeanour; you sitting here, I say, are desired presumptuously to determine, that all, all were mistaken; that the prisoner was not mad, and coercion not necessary; and this you are desired to do;—Why? Because he killed his brother! Wonderful conclusion! If any thing was wanting to confirm the evidence arising from the opinion of the family, that fatal event puts it beyond doubt. If it could be doubted whether Sir Francis too thought him totally deranged; I answer, he has sealed his opinion with blood. They had been taking precautions all night against danger and mischief from the prisoner; and, when the dreaded mischief happens, it is given you as a proof that their precautions were unnecessary; admirable logic! That they apprehended danger is clear.—Why? They have told you because they thought him mad; the mischief happens; and that which they dreaded as the natural consequence of his madness, you are to take as a proof of the soundness of his understanding.

Gentlemen, I am tired with dwelling upon this topic. The defence arising from the conduct of the family is such, that I cannot conceive what answer can be made to it. The learned Lord, I am sure, can make none; for, the argument was his own, and most sincerely do I thank him for it. For my own part, I think we have proved much more than we were bound to do; for, if there had been ten times less evidence of insanity by others, and in other respects, I think the conduct of the family would be evidence enough.

Gentlemen, this leads me to put a question to the learned Lord, of which he does not seem to be aware. He has contended that the prisoner's malady was mere melancholy and depression of spirits—that he was not mad—was in the perfect knowledge of right and wrong—knew friends from foes—and was perfectly conscious of the nature of a crime. What then must the learned Lord say of the attempt to confine him? Is he prepared to say, that Sir Francis and the family were in a foul conspiracy against the prisoner?

that

that they were attempting againſt him a crime little leſs horrible than that of which he is accuſed? Is he aware, that the priſoner's conduct would then have been completely juſtifiable? for, if there is any crime or attempt in nature, which may be repelled by the death of the aggreſſor, it is a conſpiracy and attempt to confine, as a madman, a perſon who is not ſo. The learned Lord was not aware of this dilemma; but I will relieve him from it. He never dreamt, more than I, of charging Sir Francis with ſuch a crime; and therefore he muſt concede to me, that the priſoner's ſituation juſtified the means that were attempted to ſecure him, and, if ſuccefsful, would have juſtified his confinement. I aſk no more; and, if the caſe had been my own, I would have reſted it here. But I am too much intereſted to omit other circumſtances, though not ſo material; and therefore, tired as we are, I think it my duty to proceed.

Gentlemen, I have not yet done with the impreſſion of the family; the attempt of the family to confine the priſoner, is not only good evidence of derangement in general; but what the learned Lord obſerved, of their having formerly neglected to do ſo, proves to demonſtration, that they never would have made ſuch attempt, but from the moſt overruling and cruel neceſſity. If the impreſſion of the family is evidence of the exiſtence of derangement in general, it muſt alſo be good evidence of the meaſure of that derangement: indeed the learned Lord has ſo pleaded it, and I intreat you to keep him to his argument; I again repeat, that I entirely agree with him, that the circumſtance of the family never having on any former occaſion taken meaſures for confining the priſoner, is the beſt evidence, that, in all the former inſtances which fell under their obſervation, they did not think the malady arrived at ſuch a height as to require coercion.

But what concluſion is to be drawn from that circumſtance, with reference to their conduct on the late occaſion? If they did not attempt to confine him formerly, becauſe they did *not* think him ſufficiently deranged to require ſuch meaſures; then, their attempting to confine him on the late occaſion, ought and muſt be held as good evidence that they *did then* conceive his malady to be arrived at that *criſis* (as

Fraſer

Fraſer expreſſed it) which rendered coercion neceſſary, both as the means of cure and the means of ſafety. If an argument is to be drawn from the conduct of the family, as deſcriptive of their opinions, that argument muſt be allowed to make for the priſoner as well as againſt him. The family, on former occaſions, ſays the learned Lord, did not think the priſoner *totally* deranged, becauſe they neither attempted nor intended to take meaſures for ſecuring him. The family, on the laſt occaſion, *did intend*, and actually *attempt* against the priſoner, the moſt marked and deciſive means of coercion; and therefore, they *did*, on this occaſion, conſider him to be *totally*-inſane. This is found argument and ſound ſenſe, unleſs my underſtanding too be woefully deranged.

Gentlemen, the conduct, however, of the family, becomes much ſtronger evidence of the meaſure and degree of the malady, when the nature of the diſeaſe, and the feelings of the family, are conſidered. Madneſs is a diſeaſe, which the family would not be very willing to admit, and ſtill leſs to proclaim; the fever, which was the cauſe of it, happened abroad, and ſeems to have been little known in this country; for which reaſon the family might juſtly be apprehenſive, that the world would conceive the malady to be of the hereditary kind. I ſay, therefore, it is a diſorder which you will not preſume the family would be very willing to admit; you will not preſume that they would make any unneceſſary expoſure of their friend's miſfortune, when they were ſure that the world, with a moſt uncharitable perverſeneſs, would turn his misfortune to the family's diſgrace. When, therefore, you ſee the family attempting deciſive and public meaſures againſt the priſoner, you may ſafely conclude that it was not unneceſſarily done. No ſlight, no common degree of derangement would drive them to meaſures ſo repugnant to their feelings, ſo repugnant to their intereſt. This would have been the fair preſumption, even if there had been no evidence of the feelings of the family on the occaſion; but it is not left to preſumption; it is proved inconteſtably, that the family did know and feel how deeply their honour and their intereſt were concerned in the meaſures they were taking. Sir Francis ſeems to have been particularly alive to the diſtreſſes of their ſituation. Has not Fraſer proved to you, that, when he urged him, in the garden on Monday forenoon, to ſecure the

the prifoner, (his malady, in his opinion, being then come
to a *crifis*, as he emphatically expreffed it,) Sir Francis
feemed much concerned : But concerned for what ? Was
it for the prifoner only ? No ; A good man like him
could not but feel concern for a brother in fuch a fituation. That would never have ftruck Frafer at the time,
and ftill lefs would it have occurred to him to mention
it now : but he added, that Sir Francis feemed to feel it
as a *family affront.* Thefe were his words ; and fo much
did the witnefs confider Sir Francis's concern as arifing
in part from that caufe, that he has fworn, he thought it
neceffary to expoftulate with him on the fubject, and to re-
mind him of the variegated nature of human affairs, and the
imperfect ftate of happinefs below.

And is Sir Francis the man, whom you are to fuppofe would,
within 24 hours, not only direct, but himfelf perfonally attempt, a meafure which he confidered thus to be affronting
to his family, without the moft decided and determined conviction of the neceffity of the painful ftep which he found
himfelf compelled to take ? Still, however, you fee that he
could not diveft himfelf of his feelings ; the family affront
ftill appears to have dwelt on his mind, and to have produced that fatal irrefolution, that falfe delicacy, that criminal
lenity, I had almoft called it, which was the true caufe of
the unfortunate event. We find him directing his confinement one moment, and countermanding it the next ; at one
time fending for the affiftance of the farm fervants, and then
difmiffing them on the moft equivocal appearance of abatement in the diforder, or rather on the fallacious fymptom
of a temporary calm ; and at laft, when he did attempt it,
doing it in fuch an undecided and ineffectual manner, as
clearly proves the confufion and diforder of his own mind,
and how much his feelings were ftruggling with his duty.
Had Sir Francis been as firm and determined in conducting
the attempt, as he was convinced of the neceffity of it, the
prifoner might now have been bleffing him for his kindnefs,
inftead of lamenting his lofs, and blaming his indecifion. Infatuated conduct ! unaccountable, but on the fuppofition of
a ftruggle between his feelings and his conviction : for what
elfe could make him trifle and hefitate, after he had once
taken his refolution, but his extreme averfion to incur this
S   family

family affront! But, however fatal that irresolution was to
him, however cruel to the prisoner, however much I may,
as a man, join with the prisoner in deploring the indecision
of his brother, yet, as his counsel, I did rejoice to hear it :
it proves, beyond the power of cavil or of sophiftry to ob-
viate, with what extreme reluctance Sir Francis yielded to
the advice of his friends, and the conviction of his own
fenfes : it proves how completely he must at last have been
convinced of the neceffity of coercion, before he brought
himself to attempt it : it proves that he apprehended still
greater difgrace to the family from his brother being at
large, than could arife from his confinement : it proves that
he did not attempt to fecure him, till he not only faw that
the affront was unavoidable, but that cenfure and difgrace
would fall on him, if he refifted longer the conviction of his
mind : he failed in the attempt ; but the attempt proves his
conviction, and his last breath bore teftimony to the neceffity of his conduct.

Gentlemen, were the caufe my own, I would leave it here.
I can never ftrengthen it ; I cannot forefee what anfwer can
be made to the evidence arifing from the conviction of the
family ; if there were no more in the caufe, I muft prevail ;
prevail, by the admiffion of the profecutor himself, for the
evidence arifing from the conviction of the family, was his
own argument, and I have only made the proper application
of it.

But, Gentlemen, on the part of the prifoner, we have
gone a great deal farther ; you have the cleareft proof of
the opinion of the family, and you have your notes before
you ; I defire you to fay, if either there, or in your memo-
ries, you can find one circumftance, tending even to a fufpicion, that the opinion of the family was wrong, that their
meafures were unneceffary, that the prifoner was not infane : I know you cannot ; on the contrary, I could prove
to you, that every one circumftance, which has appeared in
evidence, tends more ftrongly than another to juftify the
opinion of the family, and to prove the prifoner's complete
infanity, had the conduct of his friends been lefs convincing
on the fubject.

I

I will not weary you, Gentlemen, by detailing the evidence, becaufe, I think I fee that you are already with me; allow me only to recall to your recollection the leading circumſtances of the cafe. Firſt let me aſk you, Gentlemen, is there any thing *improbable* in the allegation that the priſoner was infane? Was he an unlikely perfon to be infane? Or was he not juſt fuch a man, as, to ufe his father's prophecy of him, would one day be confined; had not infanity become in him an habitual difeafe? Was not his fyſtem predifpofed, I think they call it, to this diforder? Had it not a moſt adequate and melancholy caufe? Will it be faid that a Weſt India fever does not often leave behind it occafional derangement? Will it be faid, that it did not do fo in the prefent inſtance? Look back upon the evidence of his brother-foldiers, who firſt difcerned the effects of the difeafe; a body of evidence, which I was not at all furprized to hear the learned Lord defire you to lay out of view. Mark the progrefs of the diforder; has it not been proved, that his family and friends thought it growing on him? Did it not once before end in confinement? and is it fo extraordinary that it ſhould end in it again? Is it not natural, nay, is it not proved to you, that repeated attacks of infanity weaken and unhinge the mind? Is it not known, that the mind in that ſtate preys upon itfelf, and that every attack of the diforder is in itfelf, in fome degree, a caufe of its return? Are you furprifed to find infanity, even without a caufe, in one who had been occafionally fubject to it? Are you furprifed to find a total infanity, in one who had been often partially deranged? But has not the caufe of the prefent attack been proved; or, at leaſt, has it not been traced back to a ſtroke which his mind had very lately received? Within lefs than two months of the accident he had loſt his father; it is proved that he loved him with the moſt filial piety; it is proved that he paid him uncommon attention during his laſt illnefs; it is proved that he was extremely affected by his death. Were it neceffary, I might argue that this is no trifling ingredient in this caufe; a man who has ſhown fuch warmth of affection for an aged parent, at a time when thofe inſtincts are fuppofed to be much effaced, is not the man, whom, in two ſhort months, you would expect to find the wiltul murderer of his brother. I have no occafion, however, for an argument like this,

this, and therefore shall not dwell upon it; but it is proved that he was uncommonly affected by his father's death: Gentlemen, we have all suffered the loss of dear relations; I hope we too have felt all that nature ought to feel. But, we met those afflictions with sound minds and vigorous understandings; we were capable of receiving the consolations of business, of philosophy, and of religion, and of allowing them all their proper force; we gradually resumed our relish for friendship and society, and were comforted: but can any of us pretend to say, what effects such afflictions might have had upon us, if we had met them with a mind, weakened, unhinged, and shattered by previous calamity? had insanity been lurking in our system, can we say, that such affliction might not have called it into action? That it did so with the prisoner, is proved beyond a doubt: It produced, at first, as was most natural, uncommon depression of spirits, not mere ordinary grief, but what the prosecutor himself admitted, did amount to real, but partial derangement; this was followed by an uncommon agitation of the nervous system, not arising from intoxication (as it seemed once attempted to be proved, though it has been since abandoned,) but from the progress of his distemper; this was accompanied with a restlessness, an incapacity to remain any time in one place, and a desire to wander and hurry about, which would of course increase the agitation and irritability of the system, till, by a complication of causes, it ended in the delirium and insanity which is our present defence. Is there any thing unnatural in this? Does the effect not correspond with the cause? Is not the *disorder* just what you would have expected, from a mind so previously unhinged? Were not the *consequences* just what you would have expected from a mind so totally deranged? His friends and family thought him dangerous both to himself and others; had the mischief happened to himself, as it is too plain he intended, who would have been surprised? But is it less surprising that it should happen to another? *Both* were *equally* dreaded by his family; else why bolt their doors, and why so much preparation of assistance when it was resolved to seize him? The friends apprehended danger from his insanity, and when the danger happens, which they dreaded, it is given you as evidence that their fears were vain; amazing conclusion! That the very circumstance, which, if there

were

were any doubt of his infanity, is of itfelf almoft enough to prove it, fhould be confidered as throwing doubt and perplexity on a cafe, in which every foul concerned has told you that they had none ; every witnefs who faw him recently before have told you, that they dreaded mifchief from his infanity ; the mifchief happens, and then the infanity is denied !

I think, then, Gentlemen, I have fhown, that the opinion of his family is completely corroborated by the probabilities of the cafe ; and that both the diforder itfelf, and the fatal effects of it, are exactly fuch as were to be expected from the previous habits and fituation of the prifoner's mind, unhinged by difeafe, fhattered by repeated attacks of derangement, and at laft fhocked by a grievous and recent affliction.

Let us now enquire, Gentlemen, if the ftate of his body, if his actions and his conduct correfpond with the opinion which his family had formed.

On the fubject of the ftate of his body, fome queftions were put at an early period of this caufe, by two gentlemen of the jury, who from thofe queftions I perceived were gentlemen of the profeffion. I am not myfelf qualified to judge, whether the circumftances they alluded to are or are not proper and decifive fymptoms of derangement. But I conclude that they are good judges ; and I defire you only to judge of the prifoner's condition by the queftions which they put. One of them put this queftion to Mr Somner, If want of fleep, and an uncommon capacity to refift the calls of hunger and the impreffions of cold, were not ufual and decided fymptoms of infanity ? Mr Somner told you, that his experience of the difeafe did not enable him to give a decided anfwer. Still lefs does mine, although I certainly have heard, that thofe are ufual and ftrong marks of madnefs. I prefume at leaft that the gentleman thought fo, who put the queftion.

Let us now then examine his fituation, with a view to this queftion, and fee what anfwer it fuggefts.

As

As to want of fleep, it is proved beyond all controversy, that this was his *constant* complaint. Mifs Kinloch has proved, that on Sunday he was wandering the whole night up and down the houfe of Gilmerton, from room to room, and tofling himfelf on every bed. When his brother and M'Millan faw him at Haddington on Monday, at the time when Somner brought him to the inn, it is proved, that when his brother afked him how he did, he anfwered, "Oh; ' Sandie, I am very ill, I cannot fleep." It is proved, that late on Monday evening, he made his efcape from them; as they were carrying him to Gilmerton ; and it is alfo clear that he had wandered in the woods all that night. It is therefore eftablifhed, that, for two nights at leaft previous to the accident, he had not clofed his eyes, befides the *constant* complaint of want of fleep, to which he had been previoufly fubject. Walker at Beanfton, indeed, feems to think that he flept fome hours while in his houfe ; I think this extremely doubtful, from the condition in which Walker found both the prifoner and his room, when he went up to waken him. But let it be held that he flept at Walker's, I will yield that to the profecutor ; but ftill it is proved, that want of fleep was his conftant complaint. It was probably both the caufe and the effect of his difeafe ; and, if he did fleep at Beanfton, and yet awoke in the outrageous ftate which Walker and Reid have defcribed, it only proves more ftrongly the fettled and ferious nature of his malady, which gained ground, notwithftanding a comfortable fleep, the moft likely and effectual means of producing an abatement. Whether, therefore, he flept or not, is indifferent to me ; if he flept, and yet awoke more deranged and outrageous than ever, the more violent and decided muft be his infanity. If he did not fleep, then it accounts for the degree and progrefs of the difeafe. But for me it is enough to fhew, that want of fleep was his conftant complaint, and that, in fact, he had not clofed his eyes on Sunday and Monday night. Follow him to Gilmerton, and you will find the fame complaint. When Sir Francis had feen him to his room, and afked him how he did, he anfwered him by complaining that he could not fleep nor reft ; and, in point of fact, you find that he was fpending that night in the fame reftlefs and agitated ftate as the two preceding, for, at

three

three in the morning, when the accident happened, he had not clofed his eyes, and was wandering through the houfe. If then, Gentlemen, want of fleep be a fymptom of infanity, as I do believe it to be, both from my own information, and from the queftion put by one of yourfelves, I think it is proved in this cafe to no ordinary degree. But I alfo believe that want of fleep is not only a fymptom of infanity, but contributes powerfully to the progrefs and violence of the difeafe; in which cafe, this circumftance acquires additional importance, and fully accounts for the diforder having made fuch rapid progrefs in fo fhort a time.

Now, as to his refifting the calls of hunger, we could have brought complete evidence on this fubject, if our fatigue had admitted of it; for, we have every perfon in waiting in whofe houfe he had been for at leaft a week before. But enough is proved, to eftablifh that one of his fymptoms was a total want of appetite. Dr Home and Dr Farquharfon have proved, that a total want of appetite was one of his complaints fome time before he left Edinburgh; and, to come nearer the fatal event, I think you have every reafon to believe, that he had not tafted food for at leaft 48 hours preceding. Mr Goldie has proved to you, that he arrived at his houfe from Dunbar about half paft three on Sunday; confequently his laft meal that day, muft have been his breakfaft at Dunbar. He refufed to eat at Mr Goldie's; and, though he afked for a little toddy, that witnefs has told you that he was unable to carry it to his head. He remained with Mr Goldie near two hours; and, before he arrived at Gilmerton, it is proved that dinner was over, that he refufed to eat, and in fact he took nothing but a little brandy and water that night. On Monday morning it is clear that, inftead of food, he had taken poifon, to counteract which, he was made to drink feveral gallons of hot water, a circumftance which would add to the debility of his fyftem. He left Gilmerton on Monday about two; and, after going half way to Edinburgh, he returned to Haddington, where Somner brought him to his brother and M'Millan, and there it is proved that he could not eat, although preffed to do it; at night he made his efcape from the chaife, and, after wandering in the woods all night,

arrived

arrived at Walker's at Beanſton about five in the morning; and Walker has proved that he had nothing there but a ſawcer full of tea; ſome toaſted bread was brought, but he could not eat it; from that he went home to Gilmerton, when it is proved, that though he once aſked for meat, he could not eat it when it was brought.

If, then, a want of appetite for food, be another ſymptom of inſanity, in what ſtronger degree would you wiſh it to be proved?

Patience of cold is ſtated as another ſymptom; do you deſire evidence of that? See him wandering all night through the houſe of Gilmerton almoſt naked; and, if that will not ſatisfy you, follow him to the woods of Beanſton, and there view him, " ſtretched out and bleaching in the northern ' blaſt."

Let, then, the Gentleman of the Jury who put that queſ- tion receive his anſwer, that patience of hunger, cold, and ſleep, are ſymptoms of inſanity, and that they concurred in the priſoner to no ordinary degree.

So far then, I ſay, that t! ¶ opinion and impreſſion of the family is again confirmed by the ſtate of the natural func- tions and appetites of the body, as well as the tenor of his mind.

Now, look to his actions and his conduct, to his demea- nour and whole behaviour, from which every profeſſional man has told you that inſanity is moſt eaſily perceived. But alas! Gentlemen, all theſe circumſtances, which made ſuch impreſſion on the witneſſes, are loſt upon us. De- ſcription fails us here; language cannot deſcribe looks, and geſtures and demeanour; there is indeed a language of the eye, but it can be expreſſed only by the eye, and, when that is not ſeen, the impreſſion cannot be conveyed. You have indeed been told of the wildneſs of his looks; but you cannot conceive this by deſcription, nor can you underſtand the *degree* of wildneſs, otherwiſe than by its effects on thoſe

who

who ſaw it, *they* believed him, from his looks, to be totally deranged, and *you* muſt believe *them*.

As to his geſtures and demeanour, turn to the evidence of Fraſer, of Walker, of Reid, and Somner. I will not follow them minutely. But you cannot have forgot Fraſer's deſcription of his loading the blunderbuſs on Monday forenoon. But ſurely the loading of a blunderbuſs or piſtols, by a perſon juſt ſtepping into his chaiſe for a journey, is in itſelf neither an uncommon nor a terrific occurrence; and yet Fraſer told you he was in the greateſt alarm, and expected every moment to ſee the blunderbuſs levelled at himſelf. What alarmed him, I ſay? Not the mere loading of the blunderbuſs. But he had marked his mad demeanour. It was his eye, his looks and geſtures, the terrible agitation of his whole frame, which was ſoon afterwards obſerved by Somner, even when the priſoner was half concealed by his chaiſe. All theſe things gave both theſe gentlemen the moſt decided conviction of his inſanity; and their opinion ought to carry conviction to you, for it is their *opinion* in this caſe to which you ought to give weight, and not to their deſcription, which can give no adequate idea of his condition and behaviour.

Recollect alſo the numberleſs circumſtances to which Somner has ſworn. Begin with the ſcene at Haddington; view the priſoner wandering from the room to the yard, from the yard to the garden, from the garden to the ſtreet, from the ſtreet back to the room, in ſuch a manner and ſuch a condition, that you ſee it was thought neceſſary to give the oſtler orders to watch him. See him next on his road to Gilmerton, whither his friends were carrying him for the beſt of purpoſes, making his eſcape from the chaiſe in the middle of a dark and dreary night. From what and to what did he eſcape? He eſcaped from his beſt friends, from thoſe who meant his good, from his only means of cure, to wander in the woods of Beanſton, and dwell with the beaſts of the field. And yet this is the knowledge of good and evil, of friend and foe, which you are deſired to believe, although I obſerved that the proſecutor never once ventured to put thoſe queſtions, after the remark which I made upon them during the examination of Mr Somner.

But let me proceed with the depofition of that gentleman. Follow him on the fatal night, and you will find his account of the prifoner's behaviour pregnant with innumerable proofs of the moft decided infanity. His perpetual reftleffnefs, his incoherent converfation, his threats to fhoot Somner at the head of the ftairs, his affection for Sir Francis at one moment, his fufpicion that he had poifoned him the next, his wandering through the houfe half naked, and laftly his frantic and outrageous geftures, when he came down to the parlour firft, when the final refolution was taken to fecure him, and again at the time of the infatuated and ineffectual attempt.

If thefe circumftances in his conduct are not thought fufficient to fupport the opinion attempt and of the family, turn to the evidence of Walker and of Reid, and you will find abundant confirmation; I will not repeat what they have told you; they were among the laft witneffes, and I faw the ftrong impreffion which their evidence made on the whole Court: one circumftance only I will mention, the vifion of the light from Heaven and the burning bufh; vifions fuch as this, are the conftant effects of a difordered imagination, and the horrors of them never fail to increafe the infanity by which they are produced.

I leave the reft of Walker and Reid's evidence to your own recollection; I am fure it made a fufficient impreffion on you, and I think I may venture to fay, that not one of you would have changed places with them, to be Lord of the Britifh Empire.

But, Gentlemen, extend your views beyond the fatal event, and you will find that the impreffion of the family continued exactly the fame; What was their firft inftinctive movement? Was it to apprehend a felon? No; It was to feize, overpower, and fecure a madman, it was to carry into execution the attempt which Sir Francis had fo egregioufly mifmanaged, in fhort it was to apply the ftrait waiftcoat, and thus, in the ftrongeft manner, eftablifhed the opinion of the family on the nature of the deed.

From his behaviour, however, after the accident, the learned Lord has drawn the only thing like an argument in
fupport

support of the profecution ; he argued, that he could not be infane, becaufe, after the event, he recollected what he had done ; but, Gentlemen, that by no means difproves his infanity. The moft complete infanity is not attended with a total lofs of memory ; elfe how could madmen remember their keeper, and thofe circumftances which make them ftand in awe of him. Nay, in fome points, the memory of madmen is moft perfect and tenacious ; they never forget an injury, they never forget their revenge ; but, Gentlemen, the recollection which the prifoner fhowed of the fatal event, muft be taken altogether, and then the argument founded on it falls inftantly to the ground. How did he recollect the event ? Did he recollect it as it really happened ? Did he recollect it unconnected with thofe frantic notions which he had previoufly conceived ? What did he fay to the fervants who feized him ? he called out to them to let him alone, for he had not an hour to live : Does not this prove that he was ftill under the impreffion, that his brother had poifoned him ? Remember too, what he faid to Mr Goldie, That he had been poifoned, and that there was a deliberate plot to murder him that night, and that what he did was in felf-defence. And yet this is the recollection from which the learned Lord would infer the foundnefs of his underftanding. Dr Monro, however, who knows a little more of infanity than either of us, gave you his opinion, that fuch groundlefs jealoufies and fufpicions againft friends and relations, was a conftant and certain mark of perfect madnefs. What the prifoner therefore faid of the event, muft be confidered more as the creation of a difordered imagination, than the impreffion of a found and fane memory. But, fays the learned Lord, we find him perfectly recollected a few days afterwards in Haddington jail ; and he feemed to treat fo rapid a recovery as impoffible. But, firft, I deny that he was perfectly recollected. He may have been fo at times ; but Dr Farquharfon has exprefsly told you that he found him often very incoherent ; As to his rapid and perfect recovery, I wonder in what part of the proof the learned Lord found that; Dr Monro, and Mr Bell, indeed, who vifited him only for a few minutes once or twice a-week, did not obferve infanity ; but they moft candidly and fcientifically told you, that this could afford no proof that he might not be often incoherent at other times ; accordingly Drs Hume and Farquharfon, who faw

him

him daily, sometimes twice or thrice, have told you that he continued to be frequently deranged; nay, did not he once behave in so outrageous a manner as to determine Major Mackay never to return to see him? did not he say so to Dr Home, as they went down the stairs of the prison? and did not the Doctor answer, that it would be absolutely necessary to apply the strait waistcoat, if he continued equally outrageous? What, therefore, could the learned Lord mean by a rapid recovery? That, in some short time, he grew comparatively better; that now, at the distance of two months, he is, thank God, as well as his grief and sorrow, and anxiety, will permit him, is true; But that his recovery was so rapid and extraordinary as to throw doubts even on the existence of his disorder, I am sure that no man who hears me will believe.

But the learned Lord, in this, fell into a manifest inconsistency; he has now argued that he could not be *very* much deranged at the fatal moment, because he became so soon well; but the learned Lord was pleased, in another part of his speech, to make a much more rapid recovery for the prisoner, than that which he has treated as impossible. He seemed very candidly to admit, that his behaviour at Walker's at Beanston was such, that, if he had committed mischief on him, it could not have been murder, on account of his insanity.—This was about six o'clock in the afternoon; and yet, by three next morning, that is in nine hours, he supposes such a rapid recovery as to make that murder then, which would have been madness at Beanston. This is a cure infinitely more wonderful, than the prisoner's recovery!

I will not, Gentlemen, dwell a instant on the case of Lord Ferrers.—It agrees in no point with this, but that the word madness occurs in both; Lord Ferrers did not fail in proving that he had been occasionally deranged, but he failed totally in proving that he was deranged at the time, or rather it was clearly proved that he was in his perfect senses; but we have not only proved previous derangement to no slight degree, but a derangement at the time, gradually increasing till it ended in a crisis of delirium; Lord Ferrers was proved to have acted from the most determined revenge, and to have laid his schemes in the most deliberate manner;

manner; while, previous malice in the prifoner here, though once attempted to be proved, is now exprefsly given up; and, as for deliberation, it is abfurd to talk of it. In fhort, while juftice and law exift, the cafes of Lord Ferrers and of the prifoner will ever be regarded as in exact oppofition and contradiction to each other.

I think I am now, Gentlemen, drawing to a conclufion. I think I have marked the great and leading features of this cafe, to which it is proper for you to direct your attention; many things I have no doubt omitted; fome indeed I have omitted by defign, for I wifhed not to diftract your attention from the leading circumftances of the cafe; and, relying on the goodnefs of my caufe, I wifh you to retire, before you are completely exhaufted; for, the founder your judgment, the more certain my fuccefs. I am indeed confident. It is not ufual for a counfel to deliver his own opinion, nor perhaps is he entitled. But the example has been fet me, and perhaps even my opinion may carry fome weight and authority along with it; perhaps alfo I owe it in juftice to the prifoner, for having once liftened to the calumnies againft him; with truth then and pleafure I can fay, that the very firft day's enquiry which I made into his cafe, effaced the prejudices I had conceived. My opinion has every day grown ftronger in his favour; and now, laying my hand upon my heart, and as I hope for mercy at the throne of heaven, I can fay, that, in my confcience, I believe him innocent.

LORD JUSTICE CLERK'S CHARGE to the JURY.

Gentlemen of the Jury,

That Sir Francis Kinloch was killed by the hand of the pannel, is proved beyond a doubt; you have therefore to confider the defence on his part ſet up. Now, it will occur to any man of ſound ſenſe and judgment, that there are different degrees of infanity.

If a man is totally and permanently mad, that man cannot be guilty of a crime; he is not amenable to the laws of his country. There is no room for placing the pannel in that predicament; for, as a perſon, totally and abſolutely mad, is not an object of puniſhment, ſo neither is he of trial.

The next infanity that is mentioned in our law books, is one that is total but temporary. When ſuch a man commits a crime, he is liable to trial; but, when he pleads infanity, it will be incumbent on him to prove that the deed was committed at a time when he was actually infane.

There is ſtill another ſort of diſtemper of mind, a partial infanity, which only relates to particular ſubjects or notions; ſuch a perſon will talk and act like a madman upon thoſe matters; but ſtill if he has as much reaſon as enables him to diſtinguiſh between right and wrong, he muſt ſuffer that puniſhment, which the law inflicts on the crime he has committed. You have therefore to conſider the ſituation of the pannel, whether his infanity is of this laſt kind, or whether he was, at the time he committed the crime, totally bereaved of reaſon. For, if it is your opinion from the evidence, that he was capable of knowing that murder was a crime, in that caſe you have to find him guilty.

Gentlemen, this is a queſtion of ſome nicety. You have the teſtimony of certain witneſſes, that he was correct and coherent in his anſwers; and you have, on the other hand, evidence that he was totally deranged by a fever in the Weſt Indies. In regard to a later period, the conduct of the family with reſpect to him, is alſo to be conſidered.

It

It has been obferved for the profecutor, that no fteps were taken to fecure him, till juft before the accident happened, whence it is attempted to be inforced, that the family thought his diforder only a fort of melancholy, and not a derangement of fuch degree as required confinement. I muft fay, that if this event had taken place eight days fooner than it did, this circumftance would have come with very great force againft the pannel; but, in the actual circumftances of the cafe, it comes with more force in his favour, and is a confideration of weight upon his fide. For, it is proved that a nurfe had actually been provided to take care of him, and a ftrait waiftcoat prepared to put on him; and pity it is that this plan was not timeoufly put in execution.

Gentlemen, I fhall not take up more of your time. You will confider the evidence well, and decide according to your confciences. If you are convinced that he knew right from wrong, you will return a verdict of guilty. On the other hand, if it fhall appear to you that he was not able to diftinguifh between moral good and evil, you are bound to acquit him. But Gentlemen, I think that, in all events, a verdict of not guilty, is not the proper verdict for you to return. I think you ought to return a fpecial verdict, finding that the pannel was guilty of taking the life of his brother, but finding alfo that he was infane at the time.

It was upon Tuesday morning about seven o'clock when the Lord Justice Clerk concluded his speech.. His Lordship proposed, that the Court should adjourn, after appointing a time for receiving the verdict : But, on a suggestion from one of the Jury, (in which the rest concurred, after conversing together in a whisper, for a minute or so,) the Court agreed to sit until the verdict should be returned. The Jury were accordingly inclosed ; and, after being absent about 35 minutes, again appeared in Court, with a verdict written out in the following terms.

The VERDICT.

At Edinburgh the 30th June, 1795.
The above assize having inclosed, made choice of the said Andrew Wauchope of Niddry Marischal, to be Chancellor, and of the said Elphingston Balfour to be their clerk ; and, having considered the criminal indictment raised and pursued at the instance of his Majesty's Advocate, for his Majesty's interest, against Sir Archibald Gordon Kinloch of Gilmerton, Baronet, pannel, the interlocutor of relevancy pronounced thereon by the Court, the evidence adduced in proof of the indictment, and evidence adduced in exculpation, they all in one voice find it proven, that the pannel killed the deceased Sir Francis Kinloch of Gilmerton, Baronet, his brother-german, in the way and manner mentioned in the Indictment ; But find it proven, that, at that time the pannel was insane, and deprived of his reason. In witness whereof, their said Chancellor and Clerk have subscribed these presents, in their names, and by their appointment, place and date aforesaid.

{ ANDREW WAUCHOPE, *Chancellor,*
{ ELPHINGSTON BALFOUR.

This verdict having been recorded, and read by the Clerk of Court, the Jury were discharged, and the Court adjourned till Friday the third of July. From that day, however, their Lordships again adjourned till Friday the tenth of the same month ; and then, on

account

account of Court of Seffion's fitting later than what had been expected, a further adjournment took place till the Wednefday following.

Wednefday, July 15. 1795.

The Court met between ten and eleven o'clock in the forenoon, when, after the ufual proclamation had been made, the Clerk of Court was defired to read the verdict of the Jury. The Lord Juftice Clerk, as Prefident, then called upon the other Judges who were prefent to deliver their opinions ; which they did *feriatim*, according to their feniority.

Lord Efkgrove. The Jury, in this melancholy cafe, have returned a diftinct verdict, by which " they, all in " one voice find it proven, that the pannel killed the de- " ceafed Sir Francis Kinloch of Gilmerton Baronet, his " brother-german, in the way and manner mentioned in " the indictment; but find it proven, that, at that time, " the pannel was infane, and deprived of his reafon." It is now to be confidered by the Court, what muft be the legal confequences of this verdict.

The crime charged againft the pannel in the indict- ment, is the crime of *murder*, which, being one of the deepeft dye, and aggravated in this cafe by the near relation between the parties, is indeed hardly credible to have been committed by any perfon endowed with the feelings and faculties of the heart and underftanding; and we have here conclufive evidence from the verdict (which is our rule) that although the fhocking deed of killing was committed, yet the perpetrator was at the time, by the will of God, deprived of that moft invaluable gift of reafon, the diftinguifhing blefling and ornament of the human kind. In this miferable fituation, could he be guilty of *murder*? I apprehend that he could not: Becaufe the offence of a crime confifts in the *animus*, and intention of the committer, confidered as a free agent, and in capacity

U   of

of diftinguifhing between moral good and evil. A human creature deprived of reafon, and difordered in his fenfes, is ftill an animal, or inftrument poffeffing ftrength and ability to commit violence; but he is no more fo than a mere mechanical machine, which, when put in motion, performs its powerful operations on all that comes in its way, without confcioufnefs of its own effects, or refponfibility for them. In like manner, the man under the influence of real madnefs, has properly no will, but does what he is not confcious or fenfible he is doing, and therefore cannot be made anfwerable for any confequences. On this ground, I am clearly of opinion, that the pannel is not an object of punifhment, and that he muft be affoilzied from the charge of murder, for which he has been tried by a moft intelligent and refpectable Jury of his country, whofe verdict neceffarily imports fuch an acquittall.

But, fhould your Lordfhips agree with me in that opinion, it will not altogether exhauft or terminate the bufinefs; circumftanced as it is. Your Lordfhips have further to difcharge the duty you owe to the country, or to the people, by taking fuch precautions for their future fafety againft fimilar violences, as your wifdom may direct, and to which your powers are undoubtedly adequate. The unfortunate Gentleman at the Bar, has unhapply been, while in a ftate of infanity, the inftrument of depriving fociety of one moft valuable member. The verdict, in fo finding, proves too well what horrid effects may flow from the depravation of reafon in a perfon living at large: and the proof, which was adduced on the part of the pannel, likewife fhows, that, during years preceding the fatal event, he was in various degrees, and at different periods, labouring under the fame kind of mental diforder, and even that (according to the obfervation of fome witneffes,) it had occafionally attacked him fince his late confinement. God, then only knows what might be the dreadful confequences of his enlargement, and being fuffered again to mix with the reft of mankind. It is your Lordfhips duty to prevent, as far as you can, a pof-

ibility

ibility of any perfon's fuffering injury by that means : and the various adjudged cafes ftanding in your records, well known both to the Judges, and the counfel, where the infanity of the perpetrator at the time of the act was found fufficient to exeem from punifhment, do all fhew, that your Lordfhips, and your predeceffors, have, in every fuch cafe, pronounced that kind of judgement, which, where I now fit, it is incumbent on me to fuggeft.

I beg leave, therefore, to propofe, that, while your Lordfhips affoilzie the pannel from the indictment for the crime of Murder, you fhall ordain him to be carried from the bar, back to the Tolbooth of Edinburgh, and grant warrant to the Magiftrates of Edinburgh, therein to receive and detain him during all the days of his life; but under this condition and exception, that, in cafe fufficient caution to the fatisfaction of this Court, fhall be found acted in the Books of Adjournal thereof, under the penalty of *Ten Thoufand Pounds* Sterling, that the pannel fhall be otherwife kept in fure and fafe cuftody, during his life, the Magiftrates, upon fuch caution being fo found, fhall be authorifed to deliver over the perfon of the pannel, into the hands and cuftody of fuch of his friends as may have given that fecurity, who will, of courfe, be entitled to receive and detain him in cuftody accordingly,

Lord Swinton. The verdict has left no room for any difference of opinion in the Court.—It has found the prifoner infane, and deprived of his reafon at the time of this fatal deed,—and therefore not guilty of the murder libelled. A perfon in the predicament ftated by the verdict is inconfcious of the difference between moral good and evil, and is not an object of punifhment. Punifhment is intended for example; but a perfon infane can have no defign; and to punifh him can be no example. The fentence of the Court, muft, therefore, acquit the prifoner from this charge.

But, after this is done another duty remains upon the Court. It is a duty not only to punifh, but to prevent all manner of evil. The fame verdict, which finds the prifoner not guilty of murder, finds it proved that he was
the

the instrument of his brother's death. Hence it is to be
presumed, that the same disease, which excited him to
that fatal action, may recur, and be dangerous to other
people. This we must prevent: and I therefore concur
with the proposal made by Lord Eskgrove, that the prisoner should be confined for life in the manner that has
been stated. It is following the course observed by the
Court in the like cases of Spence, Coalston and Blair, whose
furious fits were fatal to the lives of other people.

Lord Dunsinnan. The melancholy event which gave occasion to this trial, was accompanied, as appears from
the verdict of the Jury, with no guilt upon the part of
the pannel; and therefore can be the subject of no punishment; yet it was of such a nature, as renders it the
indispensible duty of the court, in pronouncing judgement
upon this verdict, to take such measures as may afford
full security to the public against any risk of the same sort
in time coming, in case, at any future period, this unfortunate gentleman, should by the visitation of heaven, be again
brought into the deplorable state of becoming inconscious
of what he does, and consequently not accountable for his
actions. The plan, which has been proposed, appears to
be entirely adequate to that object, and therefore has my
concurrence.

Lord Craig concured with the opinions delivered, and
thought the judgement, which had been suggested, well a-
dapted to the end in view.—And, *Lord Justice Clerk* having expressed himself to the same effect, the Clerk of Court
proceeded to write out the judgement as follows.

THE JUDGEMENT.

15th of July, 1795.

The Lord Justice Clerk, and Lords Commissioners of
Justiciary having considered the verdict of Assize, dated
and returned the 30th day of June last, in the trial of the
said

faid Sir Archibald Gordon Kinloch, pannel, whereby the
affize, all in one voice, find it proven that the pannel killed the deceafed Sir Francis Kinloch of Gilmerton Ba-
his brother-german, in the way and manner above mentioned in the indictment; but find it proven, that, at that
time, the pannel was infane and deprived of his reafon:
The faid Lords, in refpect of the faid verdict, Find, that
the faid Sir Archibald Gordon Kinloch, is not an object
of punifhment, and therefore affoilize him *fimplicitor*: But,
in refpect of the infanity and deprivation of reafon found
proven, the faid Lords decern and adjudge the faid Sir
Archibald Gordon Kinloch, to be carried from the bar,
back to the tolbooth of Edinburgh, therein to be detained
and confined prifoner during all the days of his life; or at
leaft, ay and until he is delivered to any friend or other
perfon finding caution in manner aftermentioned: and the
faid Lords grant warrant to, and ordain the Magiftrates
of Edinburgh, and keepers of their tolbooth, to deliver over
the perfon of the faid Sir Archibald Gordon Kinloch, to
fuch friend or other perfon who fhall find fufficient caution
and furety acted in the books of adjournal, to the fatisfaction of this Court, to fecure and confine him in fure and
fafe cuftody, during all the days of his life, and that under
the penalty of L. 10,000 Sterling, ; and, in the meantime,
ordain the Magiftrates of Edinburgh, and keepers of their
tolbooth, to receive and detain him prifoner, in terms of,
and agreeable to the above fentence, as they fhall be anfwerable on their higheft peril.

ROBERT M'QUEEN, *J. P. D.*

This judgement having been fubfcribed, and read, the
prifoner retired from the bar.

CERTIFICATE of CAUTION
being found in terms of the Judgement.

I ROBERT M'QUEEN of Braxfield, Lord Juftice Clerk,
hereby

hereby certify, That Doctor William Farquharfon, one
of the Members of the Royal College of Surgeons in the
city of Edinburgh, has found fufficient caution and furety, acted in the Books of Adjournal of the High Court of
Jufticiary, That he fhall fecure and confine Sir Archibald Gordon-Kinloch of Gilmerton, now prifoner in the
tolbooth of 'Edinburgh, in fure and fafe cuftody, during
all the days of his life, in terms of, and conform to the
fentence of the faid Court in all points, pronounced a-
gainft him upon the 15th day of July current. Witnefs
my hand, this 17th day of July 1795.

ROBERT M'QUEEN.

In confequence of this certificate, Sir Archibald was
removed from prifon on Friday the 17th of July 1795.

LIST

LIST of the WITNESSES cited on both Sides,
of whom only thofe marked thus * were examined.

———————— WITNESSES for the CROWN,
*of whom thofe marked thus † were likewife cited for the
pannel.*

1. Alexander Kinloch, Efq; fon of the deceafed Sir David Kinloch of Gilmerton, Baronet.†
*2. Walter Gibfon fervant to the faid Alexander Kinloch.†
*3. Alexander Menie, fometime butler to the deceafed Sir Francis Kinloch of Gilmerton, now refiding in Edinburgh.†
*4. George Douglas, fervant to Mifs Kinloch, daughter of the deceafed Sir David Kinloch of Gilmerton, Baronet.†
*5. Alexander Campbell, lately poftillion at Gilmerton, now fervant to James Drummond, Efq; of Perth.†
*6. William Reid Gardner at Gilmerton.†
7. William Temple chaife-driver in Haddington.†
*8. Dr Alexander Monro Phyfician in Edingurgh.†
9. Dr Francis Home phyfician in Edinburgh.†
*10. Dr James Home phyfician in Edinburgh.†
*11. Mr Benjamin Bell furgeon in Edinburgh.†
*12. Dr William Farquharfon furgeon in Edinburgh.†
*13. Mr George Somner furgeon in Haddington†.
*14. Alexander Frafer Sheriff-clerk to the county of Haddington.†
*15. Hugh Dods clerk to the faid Alexander Frafer.
*16. Duncan M'Millan writer in Edinburgh.†
*17. Mr Charles Hay advocate.
*18 The Rev. Mr George Goldie minifter of the Gofpel at Athelftoneford.†
*19. John Walker tenant in Beanfton.†
20. James Clerk, Efq; Sheriff-depute of the County of Edinburgh.
21. Jofeph Mack writer in Edinburgh.

22. William

22. William Scott Procurator-fiscal of the County of Edinburgh.
23. William Stephens Sheriff-officer in Edinburgh.
24. William Dumbreck hotel keeper, in St. Andrew's Square, Edinburgh.†
25. William Graham waiter to the said William Dumbreck.†
26. Charles Manderson postilion to the said William Dumbreck.†
27. James Robertson keeper of the Black Bull Inn, Edinburgh.
28. Patrick Lee vintner in Edinburgh.†
29. Alexander Murker waiter to the said Patrick Lee.†
30. Mr Alexander Hislop Provost of Haddington.
31. Mr Thomas Fairbairn Sheriff-substitute of the Shire of Haddington.†
*32. Hay Smith writer in Haddington.
33. James Stormonth writer in Edinburgh.†
34. Patrick or Peter Dickson, sometime coachman to the late Sir David Kinloch of Gilmerton, Baronet.†
35. Margaret Muir residenter in Haddington.†
36. James Robertson keeper of Edinburgh Jail.
37. Alexander Goodwin inner-keeper of said Jail.
38. James Laing, jun. writer in Edinburgh.
39. Mr Richard Somner surgeon in Haddington.

WITNESSES cited for the Pannel only.

*1. Miss Janet Kinloch, daughter of the deceased Sir David Kinloch.
*2. Lieutenant Colonel Samuel Twentyman.
*3. Captain Henry Miller of the Staffordshire Militia.
*4. Major John Mackay.
5. Mr Francis Anderson writer to the Signet.
6. Mr Alexander Low tenant at Woodend.
7. John Reid master of old Slaughters coffee-house, St. Matin's-Lane, London.

8. John

8. John Parſons hairdreſſer, No. 8. Little Suffolk Street London.
9. Margaret Curtis widow of Michael Curtis occaſionally ſervant to the pannel.
10. William Urquhart perfumer and hairdreſſer, No. 4. Panton Street, Haymarket London.
11. Mrs Margaret Hay his mother in law.
12. Alexander Urquhart green grocer London.
13. John Johnſton grieve at Gilmerton.
14. Jane Logie chamber-maid at walkers hotel, Prince's Street Edinburgh.
15. Robert Dickſon poſtilion to Mrs Fairbairn at Haddington.
16. Henry Gibſon waiter to Mr Lorimer Dunbar.
17. William Turnbull poſtilion to Mr Fraſer at Dunbar.
18. Elizabeth MacDougal hen wife at Gilmerton.
19. William Sandie driver of the Haddington coach.
20. Thomas Temple, hoſtler to Mrs Fairbairn Haddington.
21. William Moffat Forreſter at Gilmerton.
22. David Hunter labourer at Gilmerton.
23. Alexander Ferguſon labourer there.
24. Francis Buchan wright North Berwick. And
25. The Reverend Dr. David Johnſton miniſter of the goſpel at North Leith.

FINIS.